CW00707155

Fishers of Men

Phil Barber

Stoke-on-Trent
2012

Tentmaker Press
121 Hartshill Road
Stoke-on-Trent
Staffs. ST4 7LU
www.tentmakerpress.com

ISBN 978-1-901670-64-6

© Phil Barber, 2012

Unless otherwise stated, Scripture quotations are taken from the **THE HOLY BIBLE NEW INTERNATIONAL VERSION®, NIV® Copyright © 1973, 1978, 1984, 2011 by Biblica, Inc.™** Used by permission. All rights reserved worldwide.

To Suzy,

my friend, my soulmate, my love,

and to Hannah and Thomas.

A father could not wish for finer children and I am proud of you both.

Endorsements

Phil Barber is passionate about Jesus; he's passionate about bringing men and women into a life-changing encounter with Jesus; and he's passionate about growing and leading the kind of church that demonstrates the reality and relevance of the good news about Jesus to the maximum number of people in the place where he lives. I know, not just because I've read this book, but because it's been my privilege to share just a little in the life and ministry of The Potter's House. I've seen enough to testify that the story Phil tells in these 26 chapters really is true.

And he tells it with a conviction that's infectious, a sense of humour that's engaging, and an honesty that firmly faces the challenges and choices that have to be confronted in sharing the unchanging gospel in the changing culture of 21st century Britain. If you've ever been tempted to think that God has given up on his church, or if you simply want to be inspired by a story of ordinary people in an ordinary place being filled with the extraordinary power of the Spirit of God to grow a remarkable church, then read this book.

Chick Yuill, Church Life Consultant, author, and speaker

"The UK needs positive models of successful church planting with relevant approaches to communicating the Gospel, powerful worship and empowering visionary leadership. The Potter's House is one such church. Phil Barber is its outstanding leader."

Lloyd Cooke, Chief Executive, Saltbox Christian Centre

Contents

Introduction

Out of the blue

He said: 'I will make you a fisher of men.'

That was it. Short and succinct, with no preamble or explanation. It came right out of the blue, having nothing to do with the theme of the epilogue, nor with my train of thought at the time. It was not an audible voice like a whisper in my ear, nor was it merely an idea that popped into my head. Rather it was a voice that spoke deep within my being, somehow *inside* me. It was unmistakably God's voice. It is desperately difficult to describe this experience to people, but I remain convinced that it was not imagined, partly because subsequent events bear witness to the fact, and partly because at the time I was acutely aware of the Holy Spirit's presence.

The voice of God was completely arresting and the words: 'I will make you a fisher of men' repeated over and over in my mind like a ringing bell. They still do.

It was just before Christmas 1987, when I went with two friends, who were also experienced youth leaders, to take a youth weekend for the Ipstones Methodist young people. We met in Ilam Youth Hostel in the Peak District. The young people were warm and responsive, listening attentively to the messages and joining in the various activities with a great deal of enthusiasm.

Many became Christians that weekend and I hope are continuing to follow Jesus today. I love it when people (of any age) respond to the Gospel with obvious sincerity and discover the reality of a personal friendship with God for themselves.

I went to that weekend conference in the role of 'giver', to lead, teach and encourage, and yet was myself touched by the Lord in such a profound way that the whole course of my life was altered.

So it is with God.

He delights to surprise us and to exercise His sovereign power. I find it to be continually exciting to be a Christian. Life lived in the grip of the Holy Spirit is an adventure which always has a fresh twist and turn. I suppose what happened to me should be no surprise really, because I was in the role of 'giver' and it is 'in giving that we receive' (St Francis). This is one of the most important principles of love, God's nature and our Christian lives. And so I received 'immeasurably more than I could ask or imagine' (Ephesians 3:20) because I was on active service.

I have occasionally heard the comment 'why doesn't God speak to me in the way He seems to in testimony type books?' I guess the answer is that the Holy Spirit moves most powerfully in the lives of Christians when we are busily serving God on the front lines. The Bible promises, for example, that we will be given the words to say when we are testifying for Christ. Logically, if we never place ourselves in a witnessing situation, God will not have cause to give us those words. So that experience remains a mystery to us. When we give, we receive.

So what happened to me on that youth weekend?

The moment came late on Saturday night when Carly, one of the young people was leading a short epilogue. I cannot clearly remember what her theme was, but shortly after she began speaking the Lord spoke to me saying 'I will make you a fisher of men.'

Later that night my mind was flooded with all sorts of questions:

Was that really God speaking? Or is that just an over-active imagination?

What does He mean by 'I will make you'? I thought I was already a fisher of men. A bit of a reality check here!

Why has God spoken to me at this point in my life? I am feeling pretty good about things. I am in a great church, helping to lead a fruitful youth work. Why is God upsetting the applecart?

What does He want me to do...in practical terms?

What is going on, God?

As I lay in bed that night, pondering these thoughts, two Bible stories came to the fore in my mind.

Firstly, there was Elijah's moment in the cave on Mount Horeb when God's voice came to him as a *'gentle whisper'* (1 Kings 19:11-13 NIV). It seemed that his experience was similar to mine. I thought that the Bible was saying that, although God is awesome and powerful, on this occasion He did not come to Elijah in the wind, earthquake and fire, but in a more intimate, inner experience. Elijah responded to God. He got up and went to see what God wanted. He went to the mouth of the cave which implied that he was making himself available to do whatever God asked. This seemed to me to be the appropriate response for me. So I prayed: 'Here am I, Lord, send me.'

Secondly, I thought about the occasion when Jesus called the first disciples. He used the same words: *'Come follow me and I will make you fishers of men.'* (Mark 1:17 NIV) They did leave their nets and follow Him, and so began for them the greatest adventure of all. They had a few years of training on the job with Jesus and then it was literally their turn. Jesus said that he was leaving the Holy Spirit to be alongside them and to be their power, but the church would stand or fall on their testimony alone.

I thought that it was the same for me. God had spoken to me and so a new chapter was beginning; a new adventure with the Holy Spirit. 'I will make you' implied a period of preparation and training lay ahead for me, but at that time I had no idea what, where or how that could be accomplished. That night marked the beginning of several years of searching and wrestling with God.

That is the reason for this book: to describe what has happened since that encounter in 1987 and to share what I have learnt about serving God, building church and leadership.

Chapter 1

Wrestling

By the end of 1987 Suzy and I had been happily married for over seven years. We were still a DINKY couple, though that was increasingly an issue for us. I was working in a local High School as a teacher of Religious Education, a job which I largely enjoyed, but which was not without its challenges and pressures. We were attending Swan Bank Methodist Church in Burslem, which at the time was considered to be one of the leading churches in English Methodism. It had made a marked transition during the '80s from traditional and ageing to thriving, evangelical, and family friendly. Suzy and I had both been involved in helping lead the highly successful youth group there. We had seen large numbers of young people make decisions for Christ and we were thoroughly involved in the continuing outreach and nurture programme. The Group was our life. Sunday evening worship was packed, vibrant and alive with the presence of the Holy Spirit. We were surrounded by friends and at the heart of an extensive social network. They were good times. Looking back I suspect that by 1987, at the age of 32, I was getting a little long in the tooth for youth work, though I did not feel it at the time.

It was into this busy, fruitful, contented life that God had plunged His rapier word. 'Fisher of men.' 'Fisher of men.'

I wrestled with the thought that I already considered myself to be a fisher of men. I had preached many times and led people to Salvation. My life was totally focused on Gospel work. I was sold out for Him. I thought that God's reply was that there is so much more, and that, though I had born fruit, He wanted me to bear it in greater abundance.

I learnt some important lessons during this conversation with God, not least that He is a God of more; of infinite resources; endless depths. So that whatever I might have achieved already for the Kingdom was tiny compared to that which could be achieved in the economy of His vast resource. My vine could be laden with abundantly more fruit than I could ask or imagine. I remember in early 1988 feeling a strong sense of inadequacy, not so much with my ability but with my character. I was aware of my lack of a holy lifestyle, the need for a greater anointing of the Holy Spirit and more discipline and obedience. I was not ready.

However, I knew that the Lord wished to recruit an army and He wanted warriors ready with bags packed. Was I ready? Ready for anything, whatever the cost? It is very challenging to ask yourself whether you are prepared to follow Jesus wherever he leads and whatever the cost.

One of the deep convictions I hold is that we in the Western Church have largely become complacent and lukewarm compared with our brothers and sisters in other parts of the world. While they seem to exude a passion for the things of the Kingdom even to the cost of their own lives, we generally seem content to sit back and let the church gradually fade away. I have always been challenged by the words of the Spirit to the church in Laodicea:

> *'So, because you are lukewarm—neither hot nor cold—I am about to spit you out of my mouth.'*
>
> (Revelation 3:16 NIV)

It is true, we are lukewarm, and we should be ashamed. We have acquired a level of material wealth only dreamed of by previous generations, and yet, spiritually speaking, we are poverty stricken; literally wretched, pitiful, poor, blind and naked. I am always pricked with a little pang of guilt whenever I go to my local Christian bookshop with its shelves groaning under the weight of a vast array of books, Bibles, Dvds and resources. Then I think about friends in Africa with whom we have close connections these days who have access to virtually none of this resource, but who will think nothing of spending a 'short night of prayer' (literally the whole night through) or of walking 50 kilometers to get to worship, and who have a passion for the Gospel which puts me to shame. Revelation 3 warns that God will spit the lukewarm church out of His mouth. It is my observation that since the Second World War the church in the West has been experiencing this spitting out. We have stopped preaching the Gospel, expecting miracles, worshipping and praying with passion and we have declined. We are ichabod (1 Samuel 4:21), the Glory of the Lord has departed and we will continue the sad decline until we rediscover the white hot faith of the New Testament Church. This is a reality with which the whole church in this country needs to wrestle, or there will be virtually no church left within a generation.

There are, of course, exceptions to this general malaise and during 1988 there occurred one of those unplanned events which was to be a life changing encounter for me. It was a God-incidence rather than a co-incidence. I was invited by some friends who knew nothing of my inner thoughts to spend a day with a wonderful Christian couple called Roger and Faith Forster. They were (and still are) leading an organization called Ichthus Christian Fellowship. We met at their home in South East London. They described their passion for church planting to us. Their idea was to grow a church to a certain number then divide into two congregations and grow again, divide again and so on, thus gradually spreading churches across South East London. What a vision! I was both challenged and excited by their passion and determination to spread the Good News whatever the cost. They were totally committed to winning souls into the Kingdom and actually doing something to reverse the sad trend of church closure which could be observed all over the country. My heart leapt for joy as I heard their story. The Bible says that our faith is not just a matter of words but of actions (1 John 3:18) and here was a lovely Christian couple doing the business, walking the walk, not just talking the talk, as our American cousins say. I liked it; I was inspired. Here was that New Testament zeal in action; in England!

It was through this encounter that the idea of planting a church began to form in my mind. The connection between a call to be a fisher of men and church planting is clear to me because if we obey God's call to build a bigger barn He will surely fill it.

Chapter 2

Trust

'All my life has been a road to lead me to this hour' are the words of a song written by my friend Rob Phillips in a musical about the life of John Wesley, the great founding evangelist of the Methodist movement in the 18th Century. It refers to the sense of calling that Wesley had to take the Good News of Jesus to the nation and how, looking back, he might have seen God's hand at work over the years gently nudging him in the direction he was to take. They are words with which I can strongly identify because it is clear, on looking back, that God had been preparing me for the work he was calling me to, through my engagement with youth work, preaching and as a professional school teacher. It is fascinating to discover that He has been preparing you for something and you never even knew it. I have learnt that God always sees the big picture and that I can be far too focussed on the day to day challenges of life. It is a matter of trust.

Trust is something I learnt through an important event in our lives during 1988. We had been married since 1980 but no children had come along and we had become gradually more concerned and so had begun to consult the medical profession. They delivered a bombshell. Suzy had endometriosis, which is a condition in which the lining of the womb grows outside the womb.

They would have to operate, duly did so and removed one tube and ovary. So our chances of conceiving lessened considerably.

We talked to God about this and asked for His help, for a miracle. 1988 was the year we learnt a hard but vital lesson. God is a God of miracles, He loves us and provides for all of our needs but we must trust Him. So we prayed and prayed, and the months passed one by one but with no pregnancy. It was very hard to contain that feeling of desperation which threatened to rise every time we saw a pregnant lady. It did seem to us that all our friends were getting pregnant. Of course, at such times, you do become acutely focused on the moment, all too easily forgetting the big picture. So it was a struggle.

Then in the summer of that year a friend, Mark Peel, did a very brave thing. He came to see us, later confessing in great fear and trepidation, to say that the LORD had given him a prophetic word for us which was that we would know that Suzy was pregnant before the end of the year. I admire his courage, because that is a very specific word to speak into a very tender situation. As the months passed, and Summer turned to Autumn, we continued to pray, and I think Mark grew ever more nervous. I know now that this was a lesson from God on trust in the University of life.

I also know now that God has a sense of humour.

He kept us waiting until New Year's Eve. I have a very vivid picture in my mind of the blue dot which Suzy showed me on her pregnancy testing kit. It was a miracle of God's provision and love, but he also taught us to trust Him to provide. It is a lesson that was to prove vital in the years ahead. Mark was gob smacked when we told him and I think he learnt a few things that day too.

Our beautiful daughter was born on September 15th 1989. We named her Hannah which is of Hebrew origin, and means 'favoured grace'. In the Biblical story, Hannah was the mother of the prophet Samuel. Being barren, she asked God to bless her with a child, and her prayer was answered. Hence, the name literally means 'God has graced me with a son'. In similar circumstances God had graced us with a daughter.

I learnt some important lessons through this experience.

Firstly I gained heart knowledge of the truth that **what the Lord says He will do**, He will do. Heart knowledge is a world away from mere head knowledge. It is easy to look up any number of Biblical promises, learn them and quote them. Living them out and trusting until they come true is another ball game entirely.

Secondly, I learnt that if God has told me that He is going to make me a fisher of men, then that is what He will do. When He calls, then **He will provide for all of my needs** according to His riches in heaven. Therefore, what I am led by the Holy Spirit to pray for, will come to pass. Since that time I have never been concerned about material needs such as whether we would have enough money to live on, and I have found that God has always provided just enough for our needs. Even when later I took a huge pay cut to become a full time pastor there seemed to be as much money as before and we have never gone without.

Thirdly, I discovered the **sequence in which God likes to act**, which is that He gives us a calling or promise first, then He wants us to act in obedience and faith and finally comes the fulfillment of the promise. Many general promises, of course are found in the Bible, some are more specific to our situation but in either case I know now that nothing of any consequence will be achieved for the cause of the Kingdom without faith. It's the main theme of the book of Hebrews which says that God himself created the Universe by faith. So if that is how God operates, why should we expect things to be different for us?

Chapter 3

Cost

In the archive at Swan Bank Church there is a fascinating collection of documents (now removed to the Stoke-on-Trent archive). These are society membership lists from the time of the great Primitive Methodist revival in the early 1800s. The two key characters of that evangelical movement were Hugh Bourne and William Clowes. They were both at one time worshippers at Swan Bank. The record shows a list of names, including theirs, with coded symbols against the names indicating whether people were converted, had become members and whether they were considered to be living in a sanctified state. Both men have the 'sanctified' symbol indicating that they were living a holy lifestyle. I still wrestle with the thought that some people were considered by their contemporaries to be perfect. It seems an exaggerated claim, but that maybe because we live in a time when the flame of religious zeal has generally burned low in this country, while in their day the passion for and pursuit of holiness burned white hot. Yet that is the claim that is made about these two men.

I have often thought that when the Holy Spirit was looking for some people to front the next push in His strategy to convert the nation, He found here some men who had absolutely the right heart, even though they were unsuitable in other ways. They both lacked all but a very basic education. Hugh, a wheelwright, was a member at Swan Bank in 1799. He was extremely shy and rather dour in nature. So unsuitable was he to lead a great preaching revival that it is said he would preach with his hand covering his eyes. Yet he possessed a deep, deep faith in Jesus and had developed a character to match. William was a potter who lived in Burslem and who was led to faith by Hugh in 1805. He led a dissipated life before his conversion and was well known for his heavy drinking and partying lifestyle. Just an ordinary guy, whose character was transformed by a personal encounter with the living Lord Jesus Christ. Both men became famed for their powerful, passionate preaching, and both men were chosen, despite their backgrounds, because of the character they had developed through the transforming work of the Holy Spirit in their lives.

I was far from being such a man and back in 1988 was acutely conscious of the fact. To receive a call from the Lord is very daunting because there is a cost involved in being obedient, not least that of having a suitable character. I suppose that the Holy Spirit saw in me the potential for such a character. I was reminded back then of the story of Gideon choosing his 300 warriors to face the Midianites in Judges chapter 7. The ones who were finally chosen had been through a sifting process and had proved themselves to be men of character. They were the ones who lapped their water from their hands rather than bending down to the stream, indicating that they were more alert and kept their eyes peeled for any danger. They were probably the more seasoned warriors. It led me to an important revelation that good intentions are not enough. I am guessing that in the early 1800s the Holy Spirit could have found very many willing helpers, people with good intentions, but He chose two men who had the right qualities not so much in terms of traditional education and training but in terms of character, integrity and a burning passion for souls.

It is a fearful thing to fall into the hands of the living God and the call which He placed on my life led me to some very serious assessment of my character and the realization that to follow Him would be a costly path. In Matthew 16:24 Jesus said:

> *'If anyone would come after me, he must deny himself and take up his cross and follow me.'* (NIV)

I think this is one of the most challenging verses for anyone considering obeying the Lord's call. Jesus is literally saying 'come and die with me'. Die? Yes, die to self serving ambition, selfish interests, selfish motivation and love of self. To take up the cross means being prepared to put the cause of God and the needs of others completely before your own. Such a commitment takes character. Character is built through a close walk with the Lord in all the twists and turns of life. Dying to self is the true cost of discipleship. It is a hard path to take, especially in a hedonistic age which encourages the pursuit of pleasure, comfort and ease. Walking against the tide requires spiritual muscles and stamina.

How do you do this? It's not like you can flick a switch and suddenly become selfless. Though I tried.

The Bible, of course, goes even further. At that time I was led in my thoughts to another even more challenging verse. In Matthew 5:48 Jesus said:

'Be perfect, therefore, as your heavenly Father is perfect.'
(NIV)

Does this mean that we must be perfect, or strive for perfection? How is it possible to live up to such a high standard? Were Hugh Bourne and William Clowes perfect? Was that why they had been chosen to lead the revival? How is it possible?

Under the conviction of these thoughts I remember that in the summer of 1989 I went through a process of trying to improve my character and to lead a more holy life. I was challenged by St Paul's words: *'Do not conform any longer to the pattern of this world...'* (Romans 12:2 NIV) and so I made a conscious decision to change certain patterns of behaviour. It was a well meant but rather ham fisted attempt.

I resolved to:

Speak out more forthrightly and directly about my personal convictions. I continue to try though this has always been hard for me as I am by nature a rather shy person.

To rid all impure things such as books and films from the house, which I found to be a rewarding and cleansing experience. We have stuck to this and have never consciously allowed anything impure in the house over the years.

To live a more methodical or disciplined life, at which I have not yet been successful.

To get rid of debt apart from the necessary mortgage, and to never again acquire any debt. This was a crucial decision because heavy debt would have made the later move out of teaching impossible. Debt is a millstone round our necks and we should aim to be free of it.

To simplify my interests to make more room in my life for serving God. This has been difficult as I have always preferred to dip into a wide variety of pastimes rather than pursuing only one.

To speak, do and think only pure things; a continuing battle with which, no doubt, most Christians could identify.

St Paul lists his rules for holy living in Colossians 3. It sets a very high standard indeed. As I read it, I asked myself a very tough question 'who is my life truly devoted to, myself or God?' It is a question which hangs in the air over my life to this day.

I think it is a question every Christian should ask, and keep on asking.

Chapter 4

Words

In October 1989 we took in a lodger. His name was Peter Balderstone. He had just come out of Strangeways prison (now Manchester prison) where he had been serving time for drug related offences. In prison he had encountered the living Lord Jesus and had made a decision to follow him. Subsequently he had undergone a remarkable personal transformation. It was a genuine conversion. He had been set free from addiction and from his previously destructive lifestyle. He had become a passionate Christian, an evangelist. He had been a very naughty boy, yet now was such a gentle, loving man. He is one of the loveliest men I have ever met. He came to lodge with us for a while, as a half way house, while he sorted out the practical side of his life.

Peter was full of the Holy Spirit and during his stay with us shared several prophetic words which confirmed and added to my understanding of exactly what God was calling me to do. I did not at that time reveal to Peter what I was thinking about and it was fascinating to hear very direct and pertinent words from the Lord.

In October, Peter shared this word which he felt the Lord had put on his heart for me: 'you are called to pastor the flock'. Then in November he had a vision in which he saw a gate which was opened by a key and he said that he believed the key represented church planting which would be the way God would open the gate of revival in the land. The words that accompanied the vision were also a very clear instruction 'find the key to open the gate to the Lord's provision'.

Remarkable! It couldn't be more direct. I was clearly being called to pastor a flock and to plant a church but was about to learn that faithful service in all my ways must come first, then would come the time to move to a new thing.

My inner response was a rather precocious 'right let's get to it and let's gather a group and plant in a redundant church somewhere.' This approach can have its merits but can also lead to disaster because there is always a right time to do things and a seedling that is planted out into the garden too soon is very vulnerable to a quick demise from a late frost. Of course it is also possible to miss the boat by dithering about for far too long. The secret is to catch the tide at exactly the right moment. My natural instinct is to get on with things but these words coincided with a personal and professional struggle which, on reflection, was definitely part of God's planned preparation or formation of me as a leader.

I had been teaching for just over eleven years and at the time was travelling some 30 miles to work at a school in another town. It was an excellent school but I had become rather frustrated and disillusioned in my job. I was out of sorts not so much with teaching per se, but with a style of leadership at the school which was very autocratic and controlling. This was the opposite of the style of leadership which I believe is really effective and which I employ.

Words

So I went though the experience of being at work in body, but not being there in my heart. Going through the motions but wishing I was somewhere else. It is a fairly common experience I think. It is not right or healthy, however, to be in this frame of mind, especially for a Christian.

It coincided with Peter's prophetic words and led me to think that I was not yet ready to lead a church plant. The timing was not right because my heart was not right.

I remember thinking about a very simple illustration. Fill a glass with liquid and place it on the table. What comes out? Nothing as long as it is left alone. But if the glass is knocked then the liquid in it is spilled all around. Our lives are like that glass. Left alone we can appear to be perfectly happy, well behaved and apparently of good heart, but, when we are knocked by life, what comes out of us? Anger, bitterness, cynicism, harsh words, selfishness, revenge? In my case it was cynicism. I had become critical of leadership and disillusioned with working in the place God had put me. In truth it was a good job, in a good school and I had much to be thankful for. What I was spilling all around me was not good at all.

The Holy Spirit challenged me on this wrong attitude from some verses in 2 Kings 18:5-7.

'Hezekiah trusted in the LORD, the God of Israel. There was no one like him among all the kings of Judah, either before him or after him. He held fast to the LORD and did not cease to follow him; he kept the commands the LORD had given Moses. And the LORD was with him; he was

29

> *successful in whatever he undertook. He rebelled against the king of Assyria and did not serve him.'* (NIV)

Here is a challenge to do what is right in the eyes of the Lord; to do good and not to serve the evil one; to follow the Lord in all things and obey Him at all times. Here also is a promise that whoever does live like this will be successful. It is a Biblical truth that blessings follow obedience. Too many Christians are waiting for the blessings first...if God answers my prayer, then I will... It is not the way God operates.

This was a very profound lesson I had to learn from experience. It can be extremely painful, difficult and humbling 'not to cease' to follow the Lord in all the changing circumstances of life, easy during the 'still times' when our glass is at rest, but so hard when we are being knocked around by the storms of life. Maturity, however, comes through continuing to do what is right despite everything life can throw at us. This is especially true for anyone aspiring to be a leader in the church.

As God spoke, so my heart responded. Psalm 51:10-12 says:

> *'Create in me a pure heart, O God, and renew a steadfast spirit within me. Do not cast me from your presence or take your Holy Spirit from me. Restore to me the joy of your salvation and grant me a willing spirit, to sustain me.'* (NIV)

Suzy and I prayed together and I told the Lord that He could take our lives and use us as He wished. I made some practical moves too.

I resolved to give teaching in that place, for that particular boss, my very best; to pray for my boss and love him; to be at work in spirit as well as in body; to pray obediently. It was a time of true and deep repentance leading to obedience. It is the cost of discipleship and an act of trust in the Lord my God.

God, of course, was waiting for this act of submission before He moved. Through the beautiful words of Psalm 23 I was given the assurance that he would provide, restore and guide. He said to me 'because you have been faithful in small things, you will be given even greater things'. I guess the lesson that we have to learn and then keep on re-learning in our Christian walk is that when we pray and obey, then God acts. Within a few months a job came up at a school in our neighbourhood, I applied and was successful. This was a fresh start with a boss who had a totally different approach to leadership. More importantly, the school was within walking distance, cutting two hours commuting time out of the day, and providing the platform for me to become a spare time pastor in the early years of the church we were to plant.

God is good. God provides.

Chapter 5

Struggles

Not all problems are solved as neatly as that. Sometimes God uses our struggles and our pain to teach us things. On occasion he requires us to walk through them with Him, rather than taking them away.

Rheumatoid arthritis is a condition which affects the blood. Put simply, the white blood cells which normally defend the body against infection by attacking invading germs begin to attack the lining of the joints. This causes intense pain, disfigurement and in more severe cases, disability. It is a condition which, thankfully, is much more successfully controlled now than a few decades ago.

My wife Suzy was diagnosed with rheumatoid arthritis in 1986. On reflection we realize she must have had it for a while prior to the diagnosis because she would often complain of a sensation of hotness in her knees and pain in her wrists. She began various treatments but the condition gradually worsened. By 1989 she was often quite poorly. She had been a P.E. teacher but the disease had robbed her of that already. She also had a beautiful singing voice but that too was affected. At the time this was a huge personal challenge for both of us.

For me, it was so painful to see my beautiful bride in pain. I grieved to see her gradually being disfigured by a vile disease which I was helpless to prevent. For Suzy, the pain was much more profound. We did the usual things, I guess. We wept. We prayed a lot. We cried out to God for mercy, for healing. But no supernatural intervention occurred. We were told by some well meaning but mis-guided Christians that the lack of healing was due to our lack of faith. So we summoned all our faith; went to healing meetings; had numerous laying on of hands; prayed intensely. But no supernatural healing came. All of this was going on in the background while we were both still undertaking professional jobs, nursing a new born babe and wrestling with the call God had placed on our hearts to plant a church.

Although no healing had come, God was not silent about Suzy's condition and He began to teach us some things. These were the sort of lessons that you cannot get from books. I was drawn to a verse in 2 Timothy 3:5:

'...having a form of godliness but denying its power.' (NIV)

Paul here is describing the state of the godless church in the last days. The Holy Spirit said to me that this is His view of much of the church in Britain at this time. It is part of the reason why the church is generally in decline. We have plenty of religion but no real power. Indeed, there is often denial or ignorance of the reality of God's power, of miracles and even of a belief in the resurrection. The Gospel is all too often not preached and the power of the cross denied. So there exists in some quarters a strange, flaccid, ineffective form of Christianity which is more akin

34

to social work than to the white hot faith displayed by Jesus and the early Christians. The Holy Spirit told me that Suzy's illness was a parable of the church. Her debilitating, arthritic condition which had robbed her of much of her vitality was just like the weakness He could see in the church. Just as I wanted, was desperate for her to get better, so the Lord wanted His Bride to be better. He grieved over her lukewarm state, over the decline, over the spiritual disfigurement.

I do not believe God gave the condition to Suzy to teach me this. God does not inflict people with sickness but I do believe He may use an existing situation to teach us things. It had the effect of putting a passion for the church deep within my heart. A passion to pray for and work for the restoration of a power filled church in this land. It is the sort of deep revelation that can only come through a real life experience. So I became, and am to this day, a passionate builder of church. It is, without doubt, God's best idea for the World.

On November 8th Suzy was up all night with agonizing pains. I felt so helpless. Why, O God? I started to wrestle with God in prayer. 'Lord, I believe 100% in your power to heal so why isn't Suzy healed right now?' The Lord's reply came quick as a flash in my mind. 'If your faith is as strong as you say, then quit your job, go full time working for me in the church and trust me to provide for all your needs.'

Wow! There is a judgement of my faith, or lack of it. I have read many stories about saints who have done exactly this and found that the Lord does provide. But it is one thing to read about such things, and an entirely different thing to actually do it.

35

I did not believe that God was asking me to live by faith at this time. I think He was testing me and illustrating how much deeper my faith needed to be. He is Jehovah Jireh, God my Provider. He who made the Universe is well able to supply all of our needs. The lesson here was not just about God's ability to provide but about the fact that our faith must not just be a matter of words but of actions.

In 1 John 3:18 it says:

> *'Dear children, let us not love with words or tongue but with actions and in truth.'* (NIV)

So, why hasn't Suzy been healed? The simple answer is that I do not know. We continue to battle with her gradually degenerating condition. We rely on God's strength because we have very little of our own. We identify strongly with Paul's words in 2 Corinthians 12:10:

> *'That is why, for Christ's sake, I delight in weaknesses, in insults, in hardships, in persecutions, in difficulties. For when I am weak, then I am strong.'* (NIV)

I think that when we are strong in our own abilities and resources there is a danger, especially for leaders, that we slip into pride. When we are physically weak we have to allow God to fill us with His power because we do not have our own, and we can be much stronger than we would have been on our own. Such a total reliance on God can be a very powerful testimony. For Suzy and me, it has been so beneficial over many years of ministry to be able to identify with people who are suffering. No one has really been able to say to us 'you don't know what it's like to suffer like me'. We have developed a much deeper understanding of, and empathy with those who endure pain.

We also believe that God has given us a limp like the one He gave to Jacob.

> *'So Jacob was left alone, and a man wrestled with him till daybreak. When the man saw that he could not overpower him, he touched the socket of Jacob's hip so that his hip was wrenched as he wrestled with the man.'* (Genesis 32:24-25 NIV)

Though Jacob had a physical wrestling with God, this can also be used to illustrate the sort of spiritual wrestling that people undergo. The resulting limp that Jacob received was a weakness he had to live with and is an allegory of the sort of disability we may have to bear in life which causes us to become totally dependent on the Lord.

The New Testament version of this is Paul's thorn in the flesh.

> *'To keep me from becoming conceited because of these surpassingly great revelations, there was given me a thorn in my flesh, a messenger of Satan, to torment me.'* (2 Corinthians 12:7 NIV)

It was a weakness he felt had been given him to save him from conceit because of his amazing experiences and great ability.

Suzy and I have a limp, a thorn. We wish we did not, but we press on regardless trusting in God and knowing and relying on His mighty power. We have little strength of our own, yet we see victory after victory for the Kingdom. We love the people we are called to minister to with a depth of compassion we would never have known. So in a way we thank God for rheumatoid arthritis though we do pray that the brilliant doctors will one day find a cure.

It is my belief that most Christian leaders can expect to gain a limp of one kind or another. It is the Lord's mark, and act of grace, to save us from pride and self reliance and to turn us to prayer. If we are to minister the Gospel effectively it must be from a broken, open heart, not one that is hard, arrogant or unsympathetic to the frailties and needs of others.

Chapter 6

Confirmation

God continued to speak very directly concerning church planting. On 16th November came a further confirming word via Peter Balderstone who was still lodging with us:

'You are to pastor a new church.'

I decided that even though I was in the midst of so many personal struggles, it was time to share my thoughts with a few good friends and see what their reaction would be. It is always a mistake to be an island, though I observe many Christian leaders who seem to try to work in isolation. Everyone, I think, benefits from the wise counsel of friends who are not afraid to speak the truth lovingly and especially to tell you if they think the project you are planning is a stupid idea. So I went to see my brother Brian and married couple Rob and Chris Phillips with whom I have shared many Christian adventures over the years, and I told them the full story. I shared the sense of urgency I had within me to make a bold move for the Kingdom. They vowed to pray and within only a matter of days had rung to give their support and confirm that they believed I should go ahead and plant a church. 'I' became 'we' because they also said they would join the team.

They became faithfully committed to the vision, pouring their energy and wisdom into it, and all three remain so to this day. This positive reaction was for me, final confirmation.

In that spring of 1990 Suzy was working part time and I was working full-time, we had a small baby, we were battling with Suzy's illness and I had a long commute to a job I did not enjoy. So although I had made a decision in my heart to go ahead, the timing still was not right for the big move.

Throughout the first half of 1990 God continued to speak to me. On 3rd May I was watching the Dimbleby lecture and Helmut Schmidt, former Chancellor of Germany quoted a few lines of Shakespeare, which jumped right out at me.

> **Brutus:**
> *"There is a tide in the affairs of men.*
> *Which, taken at the flood, leads on to fortune;*
> *Omitted, all the voyage of their life is bound in shallows and in miseries.*
> *On such a full sea are we now afloat, and we must take the current when it serves,*
> *Or lose our ventures."*
> (Julius Caesar Act 4, scene 3, 218-224)

Brutus is in effect saying that if you have a favourable opportunity to do something, do it or you will lose your chance. I thought immediately, there is a tide in the affairs of the Kingdom and in spite of all the difficulties I must take the tide or I will miss God's perfect timing. In my opinion there are two sides to the decision to do something for God, like two sides of a coin. On one is precociousness, the other procrastination. In the middle is the sharp edge where the tide turns and the time is right.

A little while later I went for a stroll in the park opposite my parents' home. It was where I had spent many happy hours as a boy and youth mainly playing games like tick, hide and seek and later cricket, tennis and football. It held a huge store of memories. I was almost overwhelmed with nostalgia as I looked around and remembered special moments from the past, secret places, and friends' faces. The Holy Spirit spoke directly to me: 'the past is over, a new day is beginning.' I could feel things coming to a head, to a moment when the tide would be right.

There is a story in the Old Testament which is instructive in such a time as this. It involves a group of Jews who were in exile in Persia at the time of King Xerxes. Esther, a Jewess, had become first the King's favourite, then his Queen. His other favourite, and chief official was the evil Haman who had persuaded the King to issue a decree that all the Jews, men, women and children, were to be annihilated on a certain day in the near future. The King, believing himself to be a living god, had also decreed that no one, not even the Queen, could enter his court uninvited, on pain of death.

In Esther 4:1-17 is the description of the part of the story where Mordecai, the Jewish community leader had learnt of Haman's plot and he encouraged the Jewish people into a time of deep intercession. Esther was informed by her staff of Mordecai's mourning and she sent one of her servants to find out why. The servant was told everything and returned with Mordecai's request that she go to the King to beg for mercy for the Jewish people; which she could not until he summoned her, himself. What a difficult position she found herself in. Do nothing and you probably die along with all the Jewish people; go to the King and you probably die, followed by all the Jewish people. It was her time to decide. I love Mordecai's words to her:

> *'Do not think that because you are in the king's house you alone of all the Jews will escape. For if you remain silent at this time, relief and deliverance for the Jews will arise from another place, but you and your father's family will perish. And who knows but that you have come to royal position for such a time as this?'* (Esther 4:13-14 NIV)

He is effectively saying 'you were born for such a time as this', a sentiment I identify with so strongly. There are a number of important lessons which arise from this story.

Firstly, notice that Esther and the whole people had come to a moment of destiny. What we learn is that when a people or a church come to a moment of destiny then **individuals can also face a time to decide and vice versa.** It occurred to me that the call God had so clearly placed on my life as an individual would also impact many others, over many years. My time to decide would mean others would face important decisions, choices and breakthroughs in the months and years ahead. I could not underestimate the significance of the moment or of the huge responsibility it placed on my shoulders. It would be time for many to choose the Godly path in their career, family life, Christian service and personal morality. It is a truth which extends to all who are called by God.

Secondly, this leads to an important question: 'if I am faced with important personal choices how can I be sure **which option is the Godly path?'** It is a significant point. The right choice might be to take a promotion, for instance, or to stay where you are, or even to be downwardly mobile to release more time and energy for Kingdom work. The Lord needs people in high as well as humble positions. How do you decide? Esther was faced with a really difficult decision. Do nothing and let the Jews be slaughtered or go to the King uninvited and risk execution. She made a brave decision in the end, but, before that, turned immediately to fasting and prayer. She got on her face before the Lord. It is crucial that when we face 'such a time as this', that we do the same. Proverbs 3:5 is one of my favourite verses and says:

'Trust in the LORD with all your heart and lean not on your own understanding; in all your ways acknowledge Him and He will make your paths straight.' (NIV)

Only the Lord can take us through such times, only He has the power to work miracles of deliverance. The same truth applies to us corporately. Notice that Mordecai and all the people were fasting and praying for God's guidance. So must we, when God's call is placed on our lives.

Thirdly, notice that Esther was in her God assigned place for 'such a time as this.' If she had been AWOL maybe things would have gone badly for the Jews. It is absolutely crucial that we try to **stay in our place of service and obedience,** right in the centre of the flow of God's purposes. I fear that some Christians, who have a tendency to hang around the edges of the church, attending infrequently, and not serving or giving as they should will miss God's appointed opportunity for their lives. They may completely miss out on God's higher purpose, and spend their days in the shallows, when they could have been on the high seas of Kingdom adventure.

Fourthly, Esther had to go through a 'gut wrenching' moment when she took her step of faith. Imagine what she must have felt walking past the guards into the King's court, knowing that he might not extend his sceptre and then she would be executed. She was very brave. She took a real step of faith. I believe this applies to us. **We must bravely step out in faith** when we know in our hearts that we have come to God's appointed time for our lives. I have no doubt that God will test our faith and we must be bold and strong remembering that He is with us. There may be other kinds of difficult steps to take. Suppose God asks us to get to grips with tithing, to break our attachment to money and give generously to His work and to forego our own comforts and sow into the Kingdom. Are we ready to obey?

Fifthly, Esther's **step of faith led to salvation** for the Jews. This is the good news. Remember that:

> *'God knows the plans He has for us, plans to prosper us and not to harm us, plans to give us hope and a future.'*
> (Jeremiah 29:11 NIV)

I believe that, if we prayerfully take the Godly paths which are laid out for us in the appointed season, then we will see wonderful times in the years ahead, days of harvest and multiplication, healing and restoration. The alternative is too terrible to contemplate. Do we really want to be part of a church that is in a backwater, going nowhere, simply maintaining itself?

On 15th August 1990 I read the story in Luke 5:1-11 where Jesus told the disciples to cast their net into a different place. They were doubtful and resistant at first, but when they obeyed Him they made a huge catch of fish. It is a parable for the Church. Fish in the right place, in the right way and at the right time and the fish will almost jump into the net. At heart I am an evangelist, and my desire has always been to catch as many lost souls as possible for the Kingdom. This was the opportunity that now stretched out before me.

The time had come.

So after the summer holidays I went to see John Hibberts, the minister at Swan Bank Church, to tell him my story and the calling I felt to take a small group of people from the congregation and plant a church…somewhere. I could see he was rather apprehensive at first. It is a challenge for any leader to face the prospect of a group of talented people wanting to leave your congregation and go elsewhere, especially when you have a heart to build and grow church. But John's heart was bigger than mere church growing; he was into Kingdom building, so to his eternal credit he gave the plan his blessing. He suggested that I should preach to both congregations explaining the concept and inviting people to join a team who felt similarly called. I did this on October 14th 1990, and, over the following weeks, a group of seventeen adults with their associated children, including Suzy and I, identified themselves as being ready and willing to join a planting

45

team. Of this original group, two thirds are still with us, the others either went back to Swan Bank after an agreed time to help kick start the work, or have moved away.

It may be alleged that I proceeded very slowly with the whole church plant project. Why didn't I just get on with it? In my opinion such endeavours can rarely be rushed, nor can they be divorced from real events occurring in the rest of our lives. A firm foundation must be laid if the work is to survive the testing which inevitably comes. It is not all clean and neat in real life. Rarely is it the case that God speaks one day, the next week a new ministry is started. It takes careful thought, prayer and planning to work things through. I certainly do not believe in consulting God over every fine detail of life. We generally do not need to wait for a word before deciding what to wear, eat or watch. God has already given His word:

> *'Go **into all** the **world** and preach the good news to **all** creation.'* (Mark 6:15 NIV)

We Christians should be getting on with this calling with all of our strength. However, God does specifically speak to us from time to time. He does have plans and projects in mind. He does intervene in our world sometimes. He has an adventure to embark upon, a work to accomplish, and a direction to take. Sometimes we must set the sails of our little boat and take the tide of His will and purpose to wherever it leads. When we take our courage in both hands and do this, we will find that He has gone before us and though the way may be narrow and steep there will be victory.

Chapter 7

False start

On 30th March 1991 I had a further conversation with Rev John about the church planting deal. I had a team and it was decided that we would start to meet monthly to begin to sketch out some practical details. John suggested we look at the idea of taking a group into an existing small struggling chapel to revitalize it. He had a name – Boothen Chapel – a congregation with which his family had some connections and I think it grieved him to see them gradually fading away. In some ways it seemed a good plan. If you take on an existing congregation you gain premises and kudos with the local community. The devil, however, proved to be in the detail.

As someone completely green to church planting I agreed to take a look at the idea. A group of us preachers had quite successfully nurtured a couple of local chapels in the past, preaching at most of their services and generally building them up, but this was a totally different deal. We were looking at a group of people moving in and effectively taking over the leadership and running of the church. I talked to God and again asked Him to give me some direction about church planting.

Two days later, on 1st April, Paul Kinvig, a very good friend called to see me. Paul and I had walked the path of Christian service together during most of the '80s. We had been in a Gospel rock band together, we had led youth work together, we had evangelized together and he had been with me on that night in 1987 in Ilam when God's words had started off this whole odyssey. We had literally lived in each other's pockets. Then work had taken him to South Wales and we had both moved on a bit. He knew nothing of what I was contemplating but brought me a specific word which the Holy Spirit had laid on his heart. It was some verses from Jeremiah 1:8-10:

> *"'Do not be afraid of them, for I am with you and will rescue you," declares the LORD.*
> *Then the LORD reached out his hand and touched my mouth and said to me, "Now, I have put my words in your mouth. See, today I appoint you over nations and kingdoms to uproot and tear down, to destroy and overthrow, to build and to plant."'* (NIV)

Again, amazingly apposite, and specifically, the words 'to build and to plant' leapt out. So we talked long about church planting and Paul gave me some sound advice. A new church, he said, needs a good name; achievable goals; effective communication and clear vision. These are some of the principles which have been built into what would eventually follow and remain foundational to the work we continue to do for the Kingdom of God.

As we began to get into serious planning for a move out of our church family into a new and unknown world I did experience a certain level of apprehension. The thought of leaving so many good and dear friends behind was quite painful to contemplate, it was a huge challenge to our comfort zone and settled way of life, but I knew in reality I would have to do this because you cannot live with a foot in two camps. It had to be all or nothing if we were to make a success of growing a church virtually from scratch. I challenged myself with the question 'where is my zeal for the Lord if I cannot make sacrifices for Him?' I was encouraged by verses from Mark 10:29-30:

> *"'I tell you the truth," Jesus replied, "no one who has left home or brothers or sisters or mother or father or children or fields for me and the gospel will fail to receive a hundred times as much in this present age (homes, brothers, sisters, mothers, children and fields—and with them, persecutions) and in the age to come, eternal life.'"* (NIV)

I was also reminded that Elisha destroyed his plough and killed his oxen to answer the call to follow Elijah (1 Kings 19:19-21) because without them he could not return to his life as a wealthy farmer. He effectively burned all his bridges and I knew that was what God would require of Suzy and me and the team. There is a tendency in most of us to prefer comfort, security and familiar things; to slip almost imperceptibly into a rut, but it is not the path of the church planter.

On 8th April I remember that the Lord spoke to me as I was pottering around my lovely garden, weeding the vegetable plot. He said quite distinctly: 'I want you to garden in my garden.' Since then I have gone into the garden to talk to God about the church and often it has seemed as if the changing seasons have been reflected in the shifting patterns of church life as it has progressed over the years. One of the things that has remained constant has been the necessity of commitment from the leadership team. Driving a work forward requires consistent energy, sacrifice and just plain hard work. The team that was gathering to plant had to be like Gideon's army: the alert ones who lapped from their hands and who were ready for anything. (Judges 7:1-8)

Our friend Peter, who had used us as a half way house had given a small gift when he left. In prison he had learned the art of calligraphy and had presented us with a plaque with a beautifully drawn verse which he felt appropriate for our family. It has become our family motto:

> *"'But if serving the LORD seems undesirable to you, then choose for yourselves this day whom you will serve...But as for me and my household, we will serve the LORD.'"*
> (Joshua 24:15 NIV)

Sacrifice and service are definitely the key requisites for anyone contemplating church planting.

On 30th April we met with the people at Boothen Chapel to look at possibilities. We laid out the idea of a team coming from Swan Bank to take the church in a new direction. We would love them, help them and bring new life to their chapel but we would also have a passion to grow the Kingdom. I explained that there would have to be certain conditions to us joining them:

There could be no opposition to change. So they would have to be absolutely sure they wanted us.

The old Boothen would have to effectively die and transfer to the Burslem Mission Circuit.

Most things would change. There would be a new organization, new leadership, new vision, new strategy, new style meetings, new name.

But also there would be **new life and a future** for the church.

They listened politely but unenthusiastically and I knew in my heart that they would not go for it. They were typical Methodists, lovely, Godly people, but stuck in a groove of churchmanship more appropriate to a previous generation. When a group of people become so set in their ways, it is very hard to make the changes required to escape from the rut and move forward. I understand this. Every church leadership must be constantly on their guard against slipping into a familiar, comfortable pattern and growing old together. I believe that God moves on, just as society moves on, and change should be the only constant in the church's universe.

Horatius Bonar, famous and respected author and hymn writer from the 19th Century said this:

'It is easier to speak about revival than to set about it'.

And so it proved to be. The people at Boothen were just not ready for change and decided to decline our offer.

It was during all this that events had occurred in our personal lives which God would use to change us more deeply and prepare us more thoroughly than we could have ever imagined.

Chapter 8

Agony

"I c c c can't move" wept Suzy as she lay white faced on the bed. Her arthritis had returned with a vengeance. My heart sank into my boots.

She had been so well during her pregnancy with Tom but now, a few weeks after his birth she was worse than she had ever been. During pregnancy the body releases a natural steroid which relieves the symptoms of arthritis but it is apparently fairly typical for there to be a savage flare up after the birth. Savage it was. Suzy was completely immobile and in total agony. To be honest I just did not know what to do. We had help, of course, from family and friends, and the health care professionals were brilliant. I mean I did not know what to do about life. Had I misheard God? How could we possibly go on a new adventure together in these circumstances? I felt like we were in a black hole from which there seemed no escape, no light at all. This was a deeper, darker pain than I ever imagined I would have to face. It seemed more like amputation than a limp. I can't do this Lord. How can I preach the gospel, cast a vision, drive a new church forward when my wife who is my soul mate is totally immobilized?

I did the only thing I could think to do. I just went forward and trusted God to provide for us. The eleventh commandment, we sometimes jokingly say is: 'Thou shalt bash on.' And this is what we did and still do. For me it was the hardest lesson in life I have ever learnt, but an essential lesson which has carried us through all the subsequently challenging years of triumphs and disasters, joys and pain, work and sacrifice. You just have to keep on keeping on.

Suzy writes about her experience with her illness in amazingly positive terms:

> *'GOD said, "It's not good for the Man to be alone; I'll make him a helper, a companion."'* (Gen 2:18 The Message)

Our eyes met across a crowded room........actually we were set up on a date on Bonfire Night in 1974. Quite appropriate really! Our life together has been a journey of excitement, thrills, adventure and not to mention, scary moments.

Meeting Phil changed my life on so many levels. I never realised that rice went with quiche and salad and not just in a pudding, that there were so many places to holiday in Britain outside of Rhyl and that one day I would become a church leader. We spent years together helping to lead our church youth group and being a part of the worship group. We had energy, we were willing to do new things for God and we were happy with our lives.

I worked at a local primary school where I was fully involved in all aspects of the school. I was looking to achieve a management role and, to be honest, I felt 'the world was my oyster.' God had put me with Phil as his companion and helper and things were good. It was easy to fulfil that role.

Waking up one morning feeling unwell and experiencing acute pain was a turning point in my life. The diagnosis of RA and the subsequent episodes of terrifying pain took my life in a direction never imagined.

I spent time in hospital after the birth of our second child, Tom, whilst the medication was changed and the disease stabilised. In hospital I had time to reflect. What sort of a helper and companion was I to Phil? How could I help to lead a church? What had I got to offer God? How would I cope with life? Did God love me?

"'We are like clay jars in which this treasure is stored. The real power comes from God and not from us.'"
(2 Corinthians 4:7 CEV)

I went on a steep learning curve. God had called me and given me a purpose and He would provide the means to fulfil this. I was so used to 'being in control', to achieving and to getting things done that I had lost sight of who I was. I was faced with the challenge of finding out what really mattered; what was most important. The answer took me a while to realise! God loves me for who I am, He chose me for His purpose and, by His Spirit I am equipped. His Grace is sufficient; how often had I read that but failed to see the depth of meaning.

There are many times when I struggle with my health and I wonder why God doesn't perform a miracle of healing. But doing His will and being the child He wants me to be keep me focused and I dig in my 'faith feet' and take another step forward on the journey.

The arthritis has changed me physically, but spiritually too; and for the better. I've discovered so much more about God, others and myself. God definitely 'hones us' for His purpose.

Suzy is very brave. She is an inspiration to us all because she always has a smile on her face and a kindly word for someone, yet she lives with a level of daily pain and disability that would overcome most people. But that is the hand we have been dealt. We continue to pray for her healing both supernaturally and through medicine and in the mean time we just get on with things, trusting in God to give us His strength and help. He has never been found wanting.

It is also quite surprising what God teaches you through the trials and tribulations of life. Some years later God gave me the following insightful prophetic word which links Suzy's condition with His view of the church in the west.

'What do you see when you look at the church in the West, Britain, North Staffs? I will tell you what I see, says the LORD.

I see a person like one who has arthritis. Who has swollen joints, stiffness and pain and who struggles even to complete the basic necessities of life. This is like my bride, the church. My bride whom I love with a passion that is beyond your understanding.

I am deeply grieved by your condition. You are riddled with unbelief, cynicism, criticism and division. I see the pain of your people, their hurts and wounds. You have allowed the devil to pierce your people's hearts with sharp and poisoned blades. You are crippled with sin and compromise. You are stiff because you lack the oil of the anointing of my SPIRIT. You are dying.

O how I grieve over you, my people. You must repent and humble yourselves and seek my face with a passion that is radical. It is time to seek the LORD.

Away with your mission strategies, your programmes and policies. Away with your full diaries. You will achieve nothing with these alone. Humble yourselves and seek my anointing says the LORD. An hour spent by your congregations in the presence of my SPIRIT will accomplish more than a life time of your own efforts.

In my love for you I have a full flask of oil to pour out over you. I am ready to anoint you with the oil of my SPIRIT. It will be a healing oil. It will bring restoration and salvation. It will bring you to life.

Leaders of the church I urge you to bring the people to the place of anointing.

Only in this way will you receive that which you seek - the restoration and revival of the church.'

Chapter 9

Plans

Following the aborted attempt at Boothen we decided to proceed with planting a church in virgin territory. I called a meeting of all the team on 19th July. It was the meeting where we began to lay the foundations of the church. We decided that we would remain within the Methodist denomination, and, though we would aim to create a new model of church, we would as far as possible fit in with the Standing Orders (the governing document of the Methodist Church).

We decided on a team approach right from the outset. It is my observation that many leaders try to conduct a one-man ministry. They do it out of a genuine, but misplaced sense of duty and commitment. It is rarely, if ever a successful model. In my opinion, trying to have a finger in every pie, to control everything and to be 'chief cook and bottle washer', is a cause of the long term illness of some leaders and in any case severely restricts church growth. I believe that the Biblical model of the 'body' is far more efficacious, and so we shared the load by allocating various areas of responsibility to different members of the team, using each person's gifts and talents as fully as possible. When there are only seventeen of you, choice is quite limited, but it seemed as if the Holy Spirit had gathered a group who had a sufficiently varied skill set to cover all the key areas required to get the church off the ground. We could certainly carry no passengers and everyone in the team was allocated a role.

We identified a range of roles that needed to be fulfilled: leading worship, music, preaching, pastoral care, evangelism, children's work, finance and administration. There are, of course, many other jobs and roles in church life but we chose these as a compromise between the people skills we had and what is needed to get a church started.

I took the role of overall team leader and have always sought to operate by equipping and empowering others. I chose the title 'pastor' because I thought it was the least authoritarian sounding name. We have discussed the appropriateness of the word 'pastor' for the title of the senior leader many times over the years but have never really thought of a better one. 'Leader' has been suggested but 'leader Phil' does not flow quite right in conversation and 'take me to your leader' would make me sound more like a space alien than a church leader! I am not a big fan of hierarchy and grand titles and really prefer to be called by my name but I suppose it is helpful for people to have a way of identifying who the overall leader is.

Our initial plans were very modest. We decided we would begin by simply putting on a morning worship experience where the Gospel would be clearly explained and proclaimed. We would eat together and celebrate the festivals as a way of attracting new friends. We also decided we would set up some mid week prayer and fellowship which would serve as the means of extending pastoral care over all the people.

It was paramount that evangelism was our primary goal. Making new disciples of Jesus Christ has got to be the mission of every church. Attempting simply to maintain what we already have will inevitably lead to terminal decline because we all grow older. It is a disease which seems to have afflicted so many churches in the West. A cure must be found or else the church will continue to fade away. Our very clear vision has always been to help people to discover a relationship with God through Jesus.

A clear mission statement was developed which is:

> 'To lead all people to become committed followers of Jesus Christ within a loving community of growing Christians.'

When you plant a church a key question is: 'how do you encourage some new people to come along?'

We decided the appropriate strategy was to make the main event, the Sunday worship, family friendly and accessible, and to hold a monthly event to which people could invite their friends. We planned to do everything we could to make our services comprehensible and welcoming to a person who has never been to church before. It is a controversial decision. Some Christians seem obsessed with serving their own needs and indulging their own personal preferences in worship. 'I want meaty teaching,' 'I want hymns,' 'I want liturgy,' 'I want a praise band,' 'I want the organ,' 'I want,' 'I want,' 'I want.' They sometimes seem to act like selfish, spoilt babies screaming for the next feed.

Here is the big question: 'what does God want?'

My overwhelming conviction has always been that He wants lost people to come into a relationship with Him, and He wants His children to be focused on achieving that end. In my opinion, church should be primarily serving the needs of those people who are not yet in it, rather than giving the feel of a private, exclusive club. It takes sacrifice to achieve this, the sacrifice of forgetting about self and concentrating on the mission.

An obvious question is 'where do we plant?' In that first meeting we identified three potential areas, all within a three mile radius of Swan Bank, and all having no other church nearby. We agreed to check out the areas and then report back on our findings to the next meeting.

Our prayer at the end of the meeting was that the Holy Spirit would identify some elders from among us, that He would guide and protect the vision and that He would help us to birth the church on rock.

We had two further planning meetings on 19th August and 9th September. I talked to the group about us being like Gideon's army which was small but ready for battle. They achieved a remarkable military victory because they worked together and closely followed God's instructions. I warned us to be prepared for battle, to have our armour on, to watch and pray and to expect the enemy to attack. I am not a person who looks for the devil under every stone but I do believe he opposes Christians who are seeking to extend the Kingdom. He only has any power when we let him because the Bible says in 1 John 4:4:

'You, dear children, are from God and have overcome them, because the one who is in you is greater than the one who is in the world.' (NIV)

I believe with all my heart that Jesus is victorious; on the cross He defeated sin, death, evil and the devil and His triumphant resurrection is proof of His victory. If we stand in faith on the victory side we need never fear the devil and he has no power over us. It is a big 'if' though and we need to be active in aligning ourselves with God's will and be diligent in our prayers. I encouraged the team to watch over their relationships, especially their marriages, to avoid the seduction of worldly things, and basically to resist the enemy. James 4:7 says:

'Submit yourselves, then, to God. Resist the devil, and he will flee from you.' (NIV)

So we proceeded carefully and prayerfully with our plans in the light of this wisdom.

Through a mixture of prayer and discussion at these meetings, we eventually identified the area of Birches Head as having potential. The area is a mixture of approximately 1200 mainly terraced houses (called the old estate) and approximately 1500 modern ones (called the new estate). The new estate, built on the summit and slopes of a hill which overlooks the Trent valley, had no church, no pub and no community buildings of any description apart from a High School. The relatively affluent population comprised of mainly young families and a large number of commuters.

I remember it was Suzy who said that as she had driven along the main road in the Trent valley past Birches Head she had seen a kind of glow over the hill and she felt that God was drawing us to that particular area. We also discussed the fact that our particular group would have more in common with the people living in Birches Head than with people in other areas. So a decision was made, Birches Head it would be.

We decided to set up in the school. At that point in time we had no inkling of what God had in store for us; we simply chose the school because it was the only possible meeting place in the whole area. We contacted the school and discovered that they were willing to rent us a room at a modest price.

The choice of location led naturally to the choice of name. We tried to find one which was non-denominational and which might prove less of a barrier to unchurched people. We chose 'Birches Head Christian Fellowship.' Looking back now it seems rather twee, but at the time it felt right and it served us well for over a decade.

Rev John was concerned that we proceeded with the full backing of the Methodist church, so he arranged a meeting with the Chairman of the District. In the Methodist denomination the Chairman literally chairs the District Synod, the regional governing body. He is effectively the minister's minister, having pastoral care and oversight of all the churches in the District similar in some ways to a bishop in the Anglican Communion or a regional superintendent in some Pentecostal denominations. The Chairman was a lovely, godly man. I remember sitting in his study pouring out all our ideas, the calling we felt to plant a church and the details of the plans we had made. He listened attentively, then turned to Rev John and said simply 'John, if Phil thinks we should do this, then let's do it.' It was the seal of approval we needed, the official mandate, the green light.

On 20th October we brought all our plans to the Swan Bank church council. I was very keen to obtain the full blessing of the people of the church before we could proceed. Occasionally I still hear whispers that we planted the church as an act of rebellion; a sort of split. I do not know where these thoughts come from, they are 'Chinese whispers' and I wish people would guard their tongues more carefully and ascertain the facts before they speak. The fact is that at that church council I quite deliberately submitted the church planting plans to them and made it clear that we would only proceed if we got their approval. A vote was taken which was unanimously in favour of the team going ahead.

The day after this decision the Bible verse in brother Brian's diary was Jeremiah 29:11, which he felt was for us:

> *'For I know the plans I have for you," declares the LORD, "plans to prosper you and not to harm you, plans to give you hope and a future.'* (NIV)

So we had our call, our plans and our mandate and a date was set for the adventure to begin...5th January 1992.

Chapter 10

Small beginnings

It is hard to convey the sense of anticipation mixed with nervousness I think we all felt as the date approached. We were very green, having no previous experience at all of starting a church from scratch, but we also carried a huge amount of skill among the team. My nerves centred around the thought that we might fail, that no one new would come and that we would have to return back to Swan Bank, tail between our legs, after a few months. I was also conscious that after all the years of prayer and planning we had come to the moment of the launch when we would have to move out of the secure base which was Swan Bank into the unknown space out there, leaving behind all that was familiar and especially all our friends. There was pain in the offering.

But launch day in Cape Canaveral is sooo exciting. What an adventure.

We decided to do a kind of dry run on that first Sunday in January 1992 just to see how setting up and clearing away would pan out and to practice the music, children's activities and so on. We met in a classroom of the school at the end of a long corridor on the ground floor and it immediately became apparent we would have to address the issue of how to welcome newcomers, help them feel at ease and find their way in. We deliberately had only the team members present and it all seemed to go without a hitch, but it became abundantly clear that doing church in a school is darned hard work. Every mortal piece of equipment has to be brought in, set up and then dismantled and removed. Rooms have to be cleaned and prepared and then put back as they were. It is not for the faint hearted. For some people on the team there was a very early start, indeed for some saints there has been an early start more or less every Sunday ever since.

In the week following we advertised in the local press that a new church was starting in the school and we pushed leaflets through every door, then we held our collective breath.

The 12th January 1992 began with an early start for the setters up. The music had been practised, the service prepared and we waited. I remember very clearly that an excited message was passed down the long corridor: 'we can see a young couple coming down the path.' Wow! In the end three completely new people came, plus a few other family members and friends and we ended up with 23 adults and 10 children. Not revival, but a sound beginning.

We had been used to worshipping in a packed out church and it felt very weird to sit together in what was very obviously a school classroom with only 30 odd others. I can claim a certain empathy now with the missionary who has gone far from home to take the Gospel into a place where no one has gone before. I know we were only a few miles away in reality, but it did feel like the other side of the world.

We were ever so nervous. I carry one vivid picture with me of that first public Sunday. One of the musicians, Jon, had taught himself to play the keyboard and had purchased his own instrument especially for the occasion and was playing it for the first time in public. I sat behind him and saw his knees literally knocking together. He is now our technical director…from tiny acorns…

So here we were; our little craft had launched into the unknown and I really did rejoice inwardly and my prayer was: 'Lord, bless your work.'

By the 9th of February our little company had grown to 45 and the largish classroom was quite full. I put this early growth spurt down to a combination of the energy of the team and the work of the Holy Spirit. After this initial spurt numbers would stabilize and we would see a more gradual increase. People sometimes wonder why we have such a concern for numbers and why the careful noting of the exact numbers attending. There are three reasons. Firstly, I can identify a feeling of vulnerability which you experience during the initial phase which is assuaged by the comfort of knowing that numbers are increasing. The old joke that church planters tend to count everyone including the spiders has a ring of truth. Secondly, numbers do matter. We must get more bums on seats in churches in this country, it is an urgent mission. Thirdly, careful counting is important because Christians need to avoid the 'evangelastic' of over optimistic estimating. It is a lie and it leads to an unrealistic assessment of where a particular church is at. Recently someone from another church visited one of our services and said: 'ooh, there must be five hundred people here.' No, there were actually about two hundred and sixty present. So we have always been very careful to count our numbers exactly.

In the service that day a prophetic word was given by one of the new guys, John Phillips. It is based around Zechariah 4:6:

> *'Do not despise this small beginning for the eyes of the Lord rejoice to see the work begin. Not by might nor by power, but by my Spirit says the Lord.'* (NIV)

It is a word from which I drew a lot of comfort and encouragement in those early days.

To this was added another a few weeks later by Chris Phillips (no relation to John), one of the team. It was a quote from Galatians 6:9:

> *'Let us not become weary in **doing good**, for at the proper time we **will reap** a harvest if we do **not give up**.'* (NIV)

This particular verse has become a 'life scripture' for me. I have returned to it time and again, especially when the going has been tough, as it often has. I have prayed over it, and repeated it again and again. It is a spur to fight the good fight, to continue and never give up, to press on relentlessly with the calling which God has placed on our lives. It is also the truth, and we have proved it numerous times, because when we have done the good, relevant, well planned and thought out things, there has always been a harvest when we have persisted. Achieving a break through in Kingdom work has always seemed to me to be like trying to break through the tough crust of a steak pie. You persist in burrowing away and eventually the juicy, tasty reward is revealed. The trick is to keep on digging.

Chapter 11

Milestones

The phone rang early in the morning when we were still asleep. That kind of call still makes my tummy turn over because it usually heralds bad news. The worried voice on the other end said: 'We've got a problem Phil; there's been a fire at the school, you'd better get over.' I dressed hurriedly and drove over to find a badly smoke damaged but not irreparably burnt school building. It had been a deliberate arson attempt but thankfully the fire had not properly caught hold before the fire brigade had arrived. One thing was clear though - we would not be able to meet there for some considerable time. What to do? A few quick phone conversations with other leaders elicited the idea that we should approach Dave Law, a relatively new member of the church, who was Deputy Head of a nearby primary school. His response was warm and supportive and after a conversation with his Head Teacher we were offered the use of their school hall until the High School was fixed. So we moved down the hill. It is a fascinating thought that Dave just happened to be in our congregation at the right time. Another God-incidence I am sure.

My initial thought had been that this was a potential disaster to be managed and we would have to make the best of things. Strangely, it turned out to be a real blessing. Faced with adversity, everyone pulled together, we were galvanised into a burst of creative energy and the church grew rapidly. I can't quite put my finger on why the new people came or where they came from. Grace under pressure perhaps. I have observed that church growth is seasonal and in the right season people seem to appear almost magically, at other times whatever you try to do nothing seems to happen. It's a mystery and I have learnt to go with the flow.

This was one of the milestones which marked our way in the first ten or so years. There were others.

Within about 12 months of starting we made the big move from the classroom to the main school hall, which sat over 300. It felt at first like we were peas in a drum! But we had to make the move because we were crammed in to the classroom with people sitting on the tables along the back. There is a church growth rule which usually applies that when you get to over 80% full it is very difficult to grow any more. We had broken that rule on this occasion but it was still time to move, and within a few months we had grown to over 60 in attendance.

Although it felt strange to be in a cavernous great hall, the extra space opened up some creative opportunities for us. We were able to use a proper P.A. for the first time which improved the sound of our worship considerably. This was borrowed from Swan Bank at first and brought and set up each week by team member Rob. It was a real labour of love and a testament to true commitment. It is an illustration of what it actually costs to plant a church. We also began to experiment more imaginatively with all age worship by using the arts in increasing measure. I think this was the time when we began to understand that a visual element is as important as the audio in communicating the Gospel to people.

We did have some famous disasters, like the time we had thousands of invitations printed for the Christmas Eve carol service but discovered just before they were due to be posted into every house in the area that they had the wrong time on. So in another labour of love, two of the team changed the time on each by hand. We did use a lot of literature to advertise the church activities, putting information through every door in the area four times a year. This was especially important because we had no identifiable premises of our own and were this mysterious appearing/disappearing church.

A little milestone was achieved when we became the third church in the Burslem Mission Circuit in late 1995 when about 50 people took up membership and some of the original team went back to Swan Bank. By this stage we had got over the fear of failure and had a growing sense of achievement.

The seminal moment of that period was reached in 1996 when a small group of us went to a Baptist church in Altrincham for a day conference on creating a 'seeker friendly' church. We learned all about this fairly revolutionary concept which was being pioneered by a church in America called Willow Creek. It's now old hat, of course, but at the time was revolutionary. I have a vivid memory of the 'seeker service' they presented which was based on the theme of pain. There was a video clip from Mr Bean, where he drills his own teeth, followed by a really powerful drama about the pain of a wife whose husband had left her. There was lively music and a 'different' kind of message which sought to engage the modern mindset and explain what the Christian faith had to say about facing painful experiences. The backdrop was a huge sunburst mural.

We were incredibly inspired by this experience and came back with a renewed vision to try to communicate the Gospel with people who would not normally attend church. We tried various ideas beginning with a monthly seeker service which was all presentational. We called it INTRO. We abandoned the OHP for a huge old video projector and began to experiment with visuals for the first time. I think it went down like a lead balloon with some of the congregation, maybe because we were a little too radical, and our experimental worship had no congregational participation. I think we were right, however, to try this new approach because I remain convinced that the church must always look outward not inward if it is to have any hope of continuing its existence in this country.

It was during this time of experimentation that a lot of the principles which are now embedded in the culture of our church were learnt. Such as:

- We cemented the idea of **not passing round** the offering basket.
- We tried to present the Gospel in a **dynamic, relevant and engaging style** to challenge the misconception that church is generally boring, irrelevant to modern life and mainly for old people.
- We tried to remove the style of worship which has an **old fashioned feel** and, to be honest, makes a lot of Christians embarrassed to invite their friends.
- We tried to create an environment where unchurched people would be able to **understand what was going**

on, engage with it and maybe actually enjoy the experience.

- We **embraced creativity** such as media, dance, drama, music and so on, which interestingly had the effect of attracting creative people.

These principles reinforced the central concept that church exists primarily for the benefit of those people who are not yet in it. Church is not a private club. It does not belong to me, it belongs to God. It is not there to service my personal, selfish likes, whims and needs, it is a missionary organisation set up by Jesus to evangelise the world. Where churches look inward and mainly service the needs of the existing congregation they are in a maintenance mode which will ultimately lead to the downward spiral of decline and closure. Some people are afraid that creative worship somehow waters down the Gospel. It does not. The Gospel is unchanging, it is merely the clothes that it is dressed in which change. Others are afraid that older people will be marginalised but it does not have to be like this. My own father, who never missed coming to our church, and who was by then well into his nineties was thrilled and astonished by the new style of worship and he could see how important it was to communicate the Gospel in an engaging way. He used to say to me: 'son do everything you can to get the young people into church; I don't matter.' He did matter, of course, but what a great attitude.

Another absolutely crucial milestone was the setting up of a youth group. I believe that effective youth work is the power house of a church. I am not a fan of youth clubs which do little more than engage young people in ping pong, computer games and pool.

There is nothing intrinsically wrong with this type of activity except that it generally does not grow church. Youth work needs to have as its core activity the presentation of the Gospel and the engagement of young minds with the challenge to commitment to Jesus. Social activities have their place, but not in the core event. The right kind of youth work leads to faith in Jesus, attendance at worship and growing discipleship. It is one thing to measure the number of young people in church by the number who come onto the premises for judo, scouts and the like. It is an entirely different thing to count the number of young people who enthusiastically attend worship each week.

We began our youth group with three young people and three leaders. It was all there was. Some weeks there were three leaders and only two punters. It was hard going at first but we stuck at it because the formula was right and because we knew that the following year a slightly larger group would be eligible for attendance having reached the significant age of 14. We met at first in a house, then Northwood Athletic Stadium club house for a couple of years, followed by various different church halls and other venues. We felt a bit like the Children of Israel wandering in the wilderness and I longed for us to have a settled place of our own. It felt to me like a real battle against the tide to help a group of young people to find faith in Jesus for themselves and become enthusiastic about church. I knew it was one of the crucial battles to fight and we stuck at it. Creating a peer group who felt sufficiently confident to be openly Christian and begin to invite their friends took three or four years to achieve, but we did have the right formula. It was a mixture of stimulating presentation, discussion and social activities which helped most of them one by one to accept Jesus as Saviour. Some of the young people who were involved in those early years are now in senior leadership in the church, including Paul Nixon who is currently the Associate Pastor.

At the end of the decade we celebrated the Millennium together. We booked a grand hall in a local hotel followed by lunch in the restaurant. 260 people attended that special act of worship which was a wonderfully joyous occasion and a sign of how far we had progressed in eight years.

Chapter 12

The soufflé rises

A soufflé has several ingredients which are carefully mixed together in the right proportions and then put into the oven where the magic of the rising occurs. Growing a church is a lot like this. There are key ingredients, and some things which must be studiously avoided. You can't put mustard powder into a soufflé. Yuk! It has to be the right ingredients. Similarly, to grow the Kingdom in the Western world there are certain strategies, styles and approaches which will work, and some that will not. I have always regarded Kingdom work as a partnership with the Holy Spirit where we apply our brains and brawn and He then moves in His mysterious and supernatural way to bless the work and cause it to grow. The application of the heat in the oven is an illustration of the way in which the 'dunamis' power of the Holy Spirit works to bring life and growth to our own feeble efforts.

Over the first dozen years growth was consistent. We never had explosive, revival style growth but always year by year the numbers have gradually swelled just like a rising soufflé. From that initial small group of 17 adults and their children in January 1992, by the early years of the new Millennium we had congregations averaging around 150, including adults and children. We could count about 220 people who were associated with the church and who did come to worship or an event at least once a month. It was made up of the whole range of ages, including a lot of families, young people and some senior citizens. Nearly half the congregation were under 30 on a normal Sunday, a statistic which has remained fairly consistent to the present day.

During that period there is another statistic which has caused me great joy. About 60 people made a decision to follow Jesus Christ and to invite Him into their lives. These are completely new Christians, not people who have lost their faith and are making a re-commitment. Some of these people had no previous connection with church, some had family connections with existing members, some were young people who had been brought up in church making their first time commitment, and some were people who had been worshipping in church for a long time but who had never previously invited Jesus into their lives. A dangerous assumption can be made about young people growing up in church that they are Christians simply because they come to church or attend a club of some kind. They may not be, indeed most are probably not. It can be one of the reasons why they tend to drift away in their teens. They simply have not clicked with what it means to be a Christian and have not invited Jesus into their lives. For them church attendance lacks the awesome presence of the Holy Spirit, and church going is a routine ritual rather than a revolution, and in the end they get embarrassed or bored with it. The same may be said of some older people who may have sat in church for many years but who have no relationship with Jesus at all. They have a rather nasty dose of religion but no reality. The fault lies in the lack of the preaching of the Gospel and the assumption that people are Christians simply because they are sitting in church.

In our experience, because we have never made those assumptions and have consistently presented the Gospel message, we have seen results.

I want to explain some of the things which, I believe, were significant in causing the church to grow during those years. This is not an exclusive list, nor do I make the claim that this is the only way to grow the Kingdom. Not at all; there are many ways to skin a rabbit, as the old saying goes. I present here some of the things we did which worked in our particular circumstances, in the community where we were placed, and with the particular skill set that we had on our team. There are many other strategies that can be applied in other circumstances and with variously skilled people.

These are the things which caused our soufflé to rise:

Friendship evangelism. We actively encouraged everyone, young and old, to make genuine friendships with people outside the church and find ways to bring them to a service or other activity. And I do literally mean bring. Experience shows that friendship is the key. My observation of my own life, as well as the life of other Christians, is that we tend to withdraw gradually into a closed circle of friends. I think it is generally human nature to do this. The advantage of planting a church is that we had to emerge out of our circles and we were forced to make new friends. This was initially rather sad, but then became a joyful experience as our lives were enriched by the wonderful people we met.

Children's work. This has gone by several different names, but at the moment is called 'The Lighthouse' and is staffed by

83

experienced and dedicated workers who put a huge amount of effort into the planning and delivery each Sunday. We have found that parents are often looking for good quality activities for their children and when the children are happy, they are too. It has certainly been the case that many parents have made our church their home because their children enjoyed the activities we have provided for them.

Youth work. This is absolutely central to church growth. In my opinion a dynamic, effective youth work is the power house of the church. When teenagers are becoming Christians and are active in church life, the whole church is encouraged. Though young people are the church of today, the future belongs to them. We have always invested our best resources in youth work.

Relevant means of communication and variety in worship. As the decade wore on we eventually introduced a video projector to show power point presentations and video clips; we also used drama, dance, banners, puppets and a large mural. We live in a visual age and this must be reflected in our meetings if they are not to seem quaint and out of touch to a person coming for the first time. Young people are especially sensitive to this.

Sensitivity to those who have never been to church. We took great care to avoid theological terms, which a visitor, and especially an unchurched person, would not understand and we always explained what we were doing. We tried to avoid the 'cringe factor' such as: a boring 45-minute sermon, Victorian language, a freezing cold building, in-jokes, out of tune singers or dirty toilets. The classic here is the announcement about the upcoming barn dance which

84

says: 'if you would like to buy a ticket please speak to Betty.' No one who is new knows who Betty is and they are left feeling excluded and the atmosphere created is that of a private club to which outsiders are not welcome. It is done in innocence but has the consequence of driving newcomers away.

As I have previously intimated, we did not have an offering, by which I mean we did not pass round a plate or bucket during the service. There was a retiring offering and committed members were encouraged to give by standing order. The reason for this was our strong conviction that it was a mistake to thrust an offering bucket under the nose of an unchurched friend who had been brought for the first time. It simply reinforced the prejudice that 'church is just after our money'. We wanted our worship experience to create the impression that people felt they were being given to, not taken from. It was a strategy which required the Christians in the church to take seriously their obligation to give generously to the Lord's work.

A warm welcome and loving care. We developed teams of welcomers and home visitors. This is a great way of getting lots of people actively involved in service and many have the necessary people skills to do this work. Before and after worship we tried to make sure that no new friend was standing alone and feeling awkward, which could be the crucial moment when people decided to stay or leave. It required constant vigilance.

I personally have not often got involved in home visiting. I know some pastors put great store by this, but I am of the opinion that a visit by a member of my pastoral team is just as valid as a visit from me, often more so, because many possess a far higher level of skill than me in pastoral care. There is also a danger of creating rather dependent, immature Christians who only come to church if the pastor visits them regularly and who relate more to the pastor than to Jesus.

Bridging events. This means organising events which people who do not normally go to church would feel comfortable attending, such as a meal at a local restaurant or a hike or a visit to the theatre or a barbeque. The emphasis is on making friends, and there is no overt 'Christian' content.

A constant emphasis on outreach, outreach, outreach. As I have previously suggested this must be the focus of all church life. Churches must be focussed on mission, not maintenance if they are to grow (or survive!). It is an emphasis which should permeate all departments and activities within a church.

We have prayed like never before. In my opinion maintaining the prayer life of the church is the hardest struggle of all, but the most significant battle that must be won. Without prayer, nothing will happen. Church is not a glorified social institution, it is fundamentally a spiritual activity and the Holy Spirit is not active unless we pray. People will not find faith in Jesus unless the Holy Spirit has been active in the secret place in their hearts. That activity is only released through prayer. So we have, over the years, maintained regular prayer meetings where we prayed agreeing prayers over the life of the church. Agreeing, that is, both with each other, and more importantly with the Holy Spirit, as we have discerned His will for our corporate life.

Church planting is really hard work. I have been inspired many times over the years by the countless hours of toil, commitment and sacrifice of my friends who have joined me in the work. I don't think it is really possible to grow a church from scratch without such dedication.

Holy Spirit power. Acts 1:8 says:

> *'You will receive **power** when the Holy Spirit comes on you.'* (NIV)

In the original Greek the word for power is the word 'dunamis' which is the root for words such as dynamite, dynamic and dynamo. This hints at what the Bible is telling us about what it is like to experience the power of the Holy Spirit.

Some people ask: 'isn't the Holy Spirit with us already?'

Yes, in a sense. God is omnipresent and all around us. If you have become a Christian, it is only by the working of the Holy Spirit that you have begun to follow Jesus. Of course He is in us. But, to be honest, if people ask the question, then they have not experienced the power of the Holy Spirit and they are missing something.

He was in the disciples and all around them, yet still they were commanded to wait for the power to come on them.

This is because there is an experience of the power of God which is totally life transforming and supernatural, a revolution.

It's like the difference between learning to ride a pedal bike, then learning to drive and getting a Porche or Ferrari. Or getting by on a dry crust rather than eating a magnificent banquet.

God was all around Moses, but he still saw the burning bush, the manifest presence of God and received the power to work miracles.

The Holy Spirit was certainly in Jesus, but he still received the power of the Holy Spirit when He was baptized.

We need His power. I believe that just one touch from the Holy Spirit can transform everything.

I encounter so many Christians who struggle and strive, and what they lack is power.

So we have always prayed for, preached about and hungered after the 'dunamis' of the Holy Spirit. He is free to move in our midst and fundamentally it has always been His powerful working that has multiplied our efforts, converted the lost and strengthened us when we have been weak. I guess growing from 17 to 220 in a decade could be viewed as quite dynamic, but in the end it is all down to Him, and He receives all the glory.

The next big challenge we would face would be how to provide the facilities to enable the growth to continue unchecked. If the soufflé has filled the cake tin, you need a bigger one!

Chapter 13

The fulcrum

A fulcrum is a point around which something swivels; a turning or tipping point. In the early years of the new Millennium we came to such a point. It arose out of the simple practicality that we needed a place of our own if the work was to progress in the medium to long term. The issue centred around the stark reality that the cost of a building to accommodate our vision would cost millions and we didn't have millions, or even thousands and we had no collateral in the form of a building to sell. So we came to our fulcrum, the point around which the work would swing and it would be decided whether we would continue to increase or settle back into maintenance. We were very aware of this at the time and began to seek the Lord's guidance and ask Him to provide for us.

It was during summer BBQs and other social events that we began to dream dreams. I remember standing with burger in hand chatting to my good friend Andy Leake about my ideas for the future of the church. Andy was the managing director of a local manufacturing firm who shared my passion to build a great church. We agreed that what we needed were premises which would accommodate our grand plans. We wanted to build a multi media facility and fill it with new Christians. We wanted space for lots of ministries to develop in the church, serving the needy, and bringing the love of Jesus to them. We wanted space for dance, drama, music, café, retail, sports, youth, outreach, offices....so many things. We wanted a church which would be relevant, meeting the needs of people at many levels. We wanted a place where the Kingdom could grow. We needed growing room.

God spoke very clearly to me about this flood of ideas. He said that He wanted us to create a place where church and world would mix up together. I interpreted this to mean that we should create a place that was more like a conference centre than a church which unchurched people would find easily accessible. This idea formed the core principle around which the whole project we went on to create was formed.

So we began to look in earnest for suitable premises. It was to prove to be a fruitless search, but from it we learnt some vital lessons.

As we are part of the Methodist movement which is, sadly, in decline in parts of the U.K., we could have freely obtained a redundant chapel. This would have given us a building to renovate without the huge costs associated with land purchase and construction. As we looked at some potential places, however, their disadvantages became very apparent. They were built in a different era, often crammed in between other industrial or residential buildings in the inner city, and designed to serve a style of ministry which is no longer relevant in the 21st Century. In particular, most of these chapels were built before car ownership was common. They were designed for a congregation who lived locally and walked to church. It was Andy who pointed out the lack of car parking space and I realized that we would make more enemies than friends if we clogged the local streets with cars every time we held an event. It was disappointing because it immediately ruled out many potential buildings which might have given us an affordable option.

So we moved on to look at industrial and commercial sites. There are many congregations around the country which flourish in a warehouse but as we looked around we could not find one that was remotely suitable. They were all in the wrong places; in the back corner of an industrial estate miles from any dwellings, or crammed in amongst a jumble of old dilapidated potbanks without a single parking space. These places did not 'feel' right, and I was also very conscious to avoid moving our congregation too near another church, which further limited our options. I do have to confess that I felt more than a little frustrated during this time. I held on to the hope that God had a plan but we just could not seem to connect with it.

I remember our hopes were briefly raised when a promising looking retail unit became available. It was in a perfect location near to many dwellings and situated on a slight rise overlooking a busy main road into the city centre. It was a perfect spot from which to promote the Gospel. I discovered that it had been built on the site originally occupied by Providence Methodist Chapel. Was this the one? My hopes were dashed as we toured the building. Yes, it was an excellent, highly visible location. Sure, it was a modern light airy building which could be easily refurbished and maintained, but it just was not big enough. With space for an estimated 150 seats it would give us hardly any growing room at all and, the perennial problem, there would not be enough parking spaces.

My frustration increased and as I looked around I realised that the centre of Stoke, with its tightly packed terraces and jumble of industrial buildings, was unlikely to ever provide the sort of place we were looking for. Why not move to the suburbs and buy a plot of land and build? Ok, well will the millionaires kindly step forward and deposit your six figure cheques in the offering basket? Fat chance!

It was at this point, when we felt every door had been slammed shut, that we heard a whisper that was to change everything. The school where we had been meeting since 1992 were planning a new build because they wanted to move from a split site to a single site. They wanted to build on the lower one, leaving the upper, where we met, possibly surplus to requirements. They were in the early stages of a plan to seek funds to do this. My heart lifted. Was this God's plan all along? Had He led us to plant here a decade earlier knowing that the building would eventually be vacated? It was a possibility that had never occurred to me. It seemed far too good to be true. The pragmatic, former teacher side of me thought that if the building was vacated it would be demolished and the land sold for housing to give the Authority a nice cash injection. All we could do was watch and pray and wait for the school to make its move.

The school did make a move but it was not the one we were expecting. We received a letter from them saying that they had reviewed the rental we were paying and they were going to double it to nearly £200 per week to pay for four hours each Sunday morning. I was pretty angry. How could they talk about being a school that welcomed the community if they fleeced their community? I could understand the responsibility of the governors to cover their costs but this seemed grossly excessive. Were they trying to get rid of us? I do not know. The reaction of many people in church was that we should leave and find another school that would appreciate us and accommodate us for a reasonable charge. I think many people were outraged that we should be charged £10,000 per annum for the weekly use of a hall and some classrooms which were, to be honest, in a very grotty state of repair. It felt to me like we had been plunged into a spiritual battle.

There were several voices of wisdom among the congregation. They said that we should stay and tough it out, because if we stayed, and the premises did become available, we would be the main community group who were effectively the sitting tenants. In fact, we would be the only group large enough to express a genuine interest in the building that the Local Authority would take seriously. It made sense, though it was a very bitter pill to swallow. So after much discussion and soul searching, very reluctantly we agreed to pay the increased rental. We humbled ourselves. It was a fairly audacious step of faith really, because all we had was a whisper and a hope in our hearts that God was indeed moving the pieces into place to provide for our future.

So here was the fulcrum, the point around which the fate of the ministry would swing and when we would see the miraculous provision of our God. We had arrived at a very particular moment in time, a God moment, and the word that the New Testament uses for this is *'Kairos…'*

Chapter 14

Kairos

There are two words for time in the original Greek New Testament, *'Chronos'* meaning the ordinary passage of time or clock time and *'Kairos'* meaning a moment of opportunity or days ordained by God as days of favour when Christians must play their part to the full in God's great purpose.

There are many places where *'Kairos'* is used in the New Testament. For instance in Romans 13:11, where St Paul wrote to the believers in Rome about the importance of behaving in a certain way because of the special time they were living in, it says:

> *'The hour (Kairos) has come for you to wake up from your slumber.'* (NIV)

Or when Jesus' brothers challenged Him to make a public appearance in Jerusalem to prove Himself, He said:

> *'The right time (Kairos) has not yet come.'* (John 7:6 NIV)

The *'Kairos'* time He is referring to is the Passion; the appointed time when He would go up to Jerusalem to redeem mankind.

A little later in John 12:23, He says:

> *'The hour (Kairos) has come for the Son of Man to be glorified.'* (NIV)

And then He headed for Jerusalem.

We can learn from these verses that in the affairs of God's Kingdom come certain appointed times when the opportunity is favourable for certain things to be accomplished. Times when God gives His Word to His people like the commander of an army, because He knows that the time is right. A *'Kairos'* time is a time of destiny and purpose. Notice that the outcome is not certain, that we have a choice and can easily miss the opportunity. Destiny means you are presented with a choice and you can change the future. We should not confuse destiny with fate, which refers to a future which cannot be avoided or changed and which has no place in Kingdom life.

As I pondered these things, the Holy Spirit also gave me a picture of an old grandfather clock just about to strike the hour, the moment when the gears click and whirr into position and the chimes begin to sound. He said that *'kairos'* is a time when the unseen gears of the Kingdom engage and a moment of opportunity presents itself. It dawned on me that we were in a *'Kairos'* time, when Christians must play their part to the full in God's great purpose. The fact that we had been guided to plant where we did, unaware that 10 years later the building would become available was clearly something which God had organized.

Because this was such a significant moment for our church I did something I rarely do. Before worship I privately asked God for a confirmation. His reply was swift and convincing. During the service three things happened:

Paul Kinvig, a friend who lives in another part of the country and who I had not seen for at least a year turned up. When I saw him I knew it was a prophetic moment because Paul gave me an important word from Jeremiah chapter 1 when I was thinking about planting a church back in 1991.

Arthur Wakelin, our visiting preacher that morning used the text from Ecclesiastes 3:1:

> *'There is a time for everything and a season for every activity under heaven.'* (NIV)

After the service, Alison Bladen, a member of our congregation came up to me and said that during the service she had been given a picture of a clock about to strike the hour.

This was a clear and unmistakable confirmation and I became convinced that we were beginning a *'kairos'* season, a time of destiny and a time of change, when God would reveal His purpose for us and we would have to choose the Godly path. We were in days of favour and opportunity.

To my mind returned the Brutus quote from Shakespeare and it seemed that we were again at a place similar to when we had started the church a decade earlier.

> 'There is a tide in the affairs of men, which, taken at the flood, leads on to fortune,
> Omitted, all the voyage of their life is bound in shallows, and in miseries.
> It is on such a tide that we are now afloat...'

I remember speaking to the congregation about all this and saying rather dramatically:

> 'I have made my own choice. I do not want to remain in the harbour. I want to take the tide of God's opportunity and sail on the ocean of destiny. I know I must be a God pleaser and not a man pleaser to do this. I want to take the tide of the Spirit wherever He leads.'

There is a fascinating account in Acts chapter 19 of a church which went though a '*Kairos*' time. The first twenty two verses describe the huge lengths to which Paul went to communicate the Gospel. It says that he engaged in daily discussions with people in the lecture hall of Tyrannus. His talk was persuasive and relevant. It was a huge commitment which emphasizes that we must always work in partnership with God. This human effort is then accompanied by God's supernatural activity, so that signs and wonders accompany the preaching of the Gospel. The growth of the church is hinted at, and, in verse 7, we read there were only 12 believers, but by verse 18 this number had grown to many. This suggests to me that when we seize a God-given opportunity we will see the Kingdom increase. By verse 19 the Gospel had begun to penetrate into society so deeply that occult believers were burning their magic scrolls. In fact it is astonishing to note that the value of the scrolls burnt would be around five million pounds today.

Then in verse 23 it says:

> '*About that **time** there arose a great disturbance about the Way.*' (NIV)

The word for time there is not *'Chronos'* but *'Kairos'*.

In other words all that we have just noted about Paul's mission in Ephesus; the dedication; the daily witness; the two years of graft; the penetration of the Gospel into the society; the signs and wonders; the converts burning their occult items; the rapid and miraculous growth in the church; all of that was a *'Kairos'* time.

There are many lessons that can be learnt from the account of the growth of the church in Ephesus during that time which could be applied to our church.

- 'Kairos' is not the product of my over fertile imagination. In the New Testament we have a record here of a church going through a 'Kairos' time. It is Biblical.
- The *'Kairos'* season in Ephesus lasted for several years, so we could reasonably expect that ours would not necessarily end quickly if we were bold and determined to run with it. It did seem to me that we were in the midst of opportunity of a lifetime.
- *'Kairos'* is a time of action, not waiting. It is good to wait for the Lord and sometimes He asks us to do that. It is also presumptuous and a big mistake to try to run ahead of God. However, when it becomes clear that it is *(kairos)* time for action then it is also foolish to do nothing and let the opportunity pass.
- *'Kairos'* involves a time of complete commitment to the cause. Paul held his discussions every day for two whole years, and I knew we would have to become as committed as that to achieve God's plans for us.

- In a '*kairos*' time we can expect the supernatural to happen. I think that in the West many Christians have lost touch with the miraculous but I believe that God is unchanging. He is willing and very able to perform miracles when we pray and align ourselves with His will.
- The 'Kairos' season will lead to an increase in the church. This is the most important point of all, because building projects are not an end in themselves; they are a means to an end which is to extend God's Kingdom expressly by making new disciples.

If I had interpreted the signs correctly, then we were in a '*Kairos*' time which, if we could maximize, would completely shape our future and maybe that of many other people.

In late 2002 it became public knowledge that the school were drawing up plans for their new building on the lower site and the (*kairos*) time had come for us to make our move. So we wrote a letter to the Chief Education Officer expressing an interest in the upper site. We received a friendly reply indicating that our interest was noted, and inviting us to submit our outline plans for the premises. The next stage of the adventure had begun.

Chapter 15

The Bridge

In early 2003 we formed a committee to begin work on the huge project that lay before us. It was made up of two Christian business men, Andy Leake and John Machin; four members of our church leadership team, Brian Barber, Phil Price, John Phillips and Keith Nixon; a secretary, Linda Dimelow; and me.

Our initial aim was to survey the building, and draw up plans and costing by the autumn of 2003 ready to submit to the Local Authority and grant funding bodies. The building was in a very poor state of repair so it needed a complete internal refit, though the actual structure was mostly sound. We decided early on that we would make as few structural alterations as possible, so obviating the need and huge expense of architects. We used the good offices of Andy's team of designers to draw up the refit plans. I do believe that Andy's membership of our church was no coincidence but was by God's design and he was definitely the right man in the right place at the right time. It is an illustration of the *'Kairos'* season we were in.

Basically we discovered that we would have to renew virtually everything, apart from the shell of the building. We looked at the roof, electrics, plumbing, heating, windows, plaster work, decoration, fittings, security and safety, communication...and so on. It was a huge list. We also began to approach potential funding bodies to find the ones whose funding criteria matched the plans we were forming. We realized that we would have to prove that the facilities we wanted to create would actually meet real not imagined needs, and that we would have to carefully survey the community. All this plunged us into a blitz of meetings, site visits, discussions, and visits to other projects to see what they had done. We were and remain keen learners.

In those early meetings we made some significant decisions. We decided to set up an independent charitable trust which would be called The Bridge Centre Trust. It was actually my own son Tom who came up with the name 'Bridge' which he thought encapsulated the Lord's instruction to create a place where the world and church would meet. We decided to separate the running of the project from the Church Leadership Team so that they and the pastor would be freed from the sort of premises business – leaking roof and burst boiler – which often bedevil church leaderships and divert them from focusing on evangelism. This independence would also enable us to draw funds from bodies that are reluctant to give to church projects. We employed a solicitor to begin work drawing up a constitution for the formation of the Bridge Centre Trust as a company Limited by Guarantee. We started preparatory work on an application for charitable status, set up a web site and a bank account, designed a logo and many, many other things. We also decided to employ committee member Phil Price as our part-time project administrator to cope with the sheer volume of work.

We had a tight schedule because we had to submit an outline plan to the Local Authority before the thought that they should dispose of the site to builders crystallized in the minds of City Councillors. We had to persuade them pretty quickly that our project was viable and would provide much needed community facilities. Our plan was to acquire the upper site of Birches Head High School, to convert it into the Bridge Centre and to operate it as a social enterprise for the benefit of the local community. We envisaged five elements to the project: a community centre, a centre for the development of performing arts, conferencing facilities, start up units for business and, of course, facilities for the church to continue its work of extending God's Kingdom. Central to the plan was that after the initial refurbishment the whole project would be self funding, requiring no further financial support from either public or church purses.

I want to pay tribute to the members of the committee for the huge amount of voluntary work they gave, without which the project would never have got off the ground. Some of them often worked for the project instead of working on their own businesses, and made huge personal sacrifices. It was a titanic effort! At this stage, of course, we were burning the candle at both ends with no guarantee of success. In fact the school's new build had not even been started. We had to proceed with audacious faith.

By our committee meeting on 14th July 2003 we had draft refit plans to view, and an outline business plan, showing projected build costs and an indication of what we thought would be our income and expenditure in the early years of operation. We were also preparing to approach the congregation for a financial gift to prime the project. It was at this point that tragedy struck. Our administrator, Phil Price, was suddenly taken ill. Medical examination confirmed that he had a huge brain tumour and he passed away after a very short illness. We were left stunned, grief stricken and bereft. He was our dear friend and partner in the Gospel, cruelly snatched away in an untimely fashion. Just before he died Phil said to me: 'Phil, this project is going to happen, it's a done deal.' It was a statement of faith I held close to my heart in the years ahead.

By November 2003 we had progressed to the point that the business plan was complete, potential funders were lined up, and the Local Authority were making positive noises. Andy and I had been to see the elected Mayor, Mike Wolfe who had been openly enthusiastic about our ideas. As yet it was all talk, and nothing concrete was in place. My father had taught me never to assume something was yours until your whole hand closed around it, so I remained quite tense and nervous, and tried my hardest to hold onto faith and Phil Price's words. We had done a whole year's work but so far had nothing solid to show for it apart from the church's generosity. The gift day, from a congregation of about 200, 40 of whom were children, had raised an amazing £100,000.

In January 2004 we sent out a colour brochure describing our business plan to every influential person we could think of – local Councillors, Members of Parliament, funders, officers of the Authority, the Mayor, community leaders and church leaders. Our aim was to create a momentum of opinion which would influence the decision making shortly to occur. We wanted to create the impression that the Bridge Centre project was already a done deal;

which it wasn't. We were also battling with the issue I am sure many other projects face; that of satisfying the requirements of potential funders, getting one to commit so others would follow and trying to tie in our project with their deadlines for funding spend.

And still we waited for the official nod.

I do believe that God moved in those early months of 2004 to seal the deal. We heard that the City Council had voted not to demolish the site and sell it for housing, which was a real breakthrough. Then we heard that they had voted that we would be the sole clients when the time came to dispose of the site. This was our *'kairos',* our moment of opportunity and favour. It came because we had prayed and trusted in the Lord, followed His plan obediently and put in the hard graft. It's always a partnership.

Even though at this point we had not had the final Council decision to adopt our plan and put the site into our hands, we proceeded with faith. As spring turned to summer we looked at things like planning and change of use applications. We talked to the Corporate Assets Department who would take over the building once Education declared it surplus to requirements to begin negotiations over the sale price. This was tricky because 3.4 acres of prime building land is pretty valuable and we didn't know what view they would take. Still, we trusted in God to provide.

By midsummer – deep joy – the work began on the extension to the school's lower site. One by one the dominoes were falling. Progress slowed markedly during the remainder of 2004 and into the spring of 2005 as we waited for the extension to go up. I think we learnt a lot about patience during those months.

We did finally form the limited company during the autumn of 2004 which paved the way for charitable status which was a stipulation of some funding bodies. At our committee meeting on 15th November we were informed that the school were aiming to vacate the premises by April 2005 and though this was later put back to July we could see the end game approaching.

To illustrate the immense pressure we were under during this final phase of the acquisition, one of the huge challenges we faced was the security of the building - which we did not own. The school had understandably focused all its attention on the grand new build below, and our upper site became increasingly neglected. The school children hated it; it had become filthy and dilapidated and they called it: 'that minging place.' It was insecure, and, at night, gangs of youths mainly from outside Birches Head roamed the site. There was extensive vandalism, break-ins and several serious arson attempts. We prayed and prayed that angels would protect the site. We nagged the school to close windows at night and even screwed down the vulnerable ones ourselves. We removed rubble which was being used as ammunition from around the place, and we asked the school caretaker to do a double security check each evening. Even so, I did have many sleepless nights.

The final pieces of the jigsaw finally fell into place during the summer of 2005 and the City Council agreed to sell the whole site to us for a sum of £200,000. Some people, including some local Councillors, felt we should have been given a peppercorn rent but we actually preferred to buy because it gave us the option of raising a mortgage against the value of the property. It was a generous price really, and a sign of the Council's investment in the project, because we now own 3.4 acres of prime building land and a building insured for £3.5 million. At this time we also received charitable status and planning permission, subject to a few not very onerous conditions. Although we had many frustrations with grant funding bodies we had now been promised £350,000 to which we could add a mortgage sum of £300,000. It seemed a very paltry amount and I think many people doubted we would be able to deliver the project for only £650,000. It would be a further challenge.

The school did move out at the end of July and we were granted a license to occupy the building until the legalities could be completed for our purchase. I think the period from the end of July until we finally purchased in November was the most challenging of all. The building had been left in a terrible mess, stripped of all useful items, strewn with rubbish and absolutely filthy. The church had to meet in a small hall at one end of the building, in what is now the small conference suite, which we tried to make as habitable as possible. Heating was minimal, the toilets indescribable. The issue was that we could do no work at all until the purchase was complete. So we had to stoically endure the privations, though the congregation seemed to treat it all as an adventure. The most difficult problem was that we could not yet secure the site, and we experienced three further arson attempts during those months. I do not know why the fire did not take hold on each occasion – perhaps the angels we prayed for did protect us.

At the beginning of November 2005 one other trustee, John Phillips, and I, found ourselves in the solicitor's office signing the papers to complete the purchase of the site. We celebrated with cake and coffee afterwards! We received the keys to the building on November 10th. During the autumn we had asked for another gift from the congregation and they had responded with a further act of sacrificial giving. This was a huge sacrifice by members of the congregation, some of whom went without family holidays that year. Our two gift days raised just over £200,000 in total so we were able to buy the whole site outright and pay our legal fees. An amazing God-incidence. '*Kairos*' was still in evidence.

This marked the completion of the first phase of our Bridge adventure. Ahead lay several gruelling years to get the place fit for habitation and open for business. Once you own a set of premises you immediately incur industrial sized costs, like the £10,000 we had to pay for a year's insurance. So we were immediately plunged into the next challenge - to get the building open for business and earning money to offset the costs. The roller coaster ride would continue.

I still find it wonderful to contemplate that our little group of 17 adults plus children who set out nervously, yet faithfully in 1992, had arrived, along with a crowd of new friends, in possession of such a huge project in so short a time. God has worked His wonders and we give Him the glory.

Chapter 16

21st Century church

In the midst of all the busy work to establish the Bridge project the spiritual life of the church had to continue. People still needed to be cared for and nourished with worship and teaching and new disciples needed to be created. I was very conscious that we should not kill the goose which was laying the golden egg.

During the early years of the decade we had established a small community centre on the high street in the old part of Birches Head. It was a small shop which we rented from the owner of the hardware store next door. It had a living room sized main room, galley kitchen and toilet down stairs and two small meeting rooms upstairs. Our refit of this small premises was to be a rehearsal for the main deal we were now involved in. We called it The Potters House and we tried to establish it as a modest community centre for the area. Although I think we had mixed success in developing our community work from this place, it did give us a base to work from and enabled us to employ two more staff: a community worker and a youth worker. It was a very significant step for a church which had no premises at all to have a place in which to pray, meet and from which to conduct outreach. It was here, for example, that our community worker, Lynne, began to develop the counselling and mercy work that is now called Family

Support Services and which is now such a significant part of the church's work.

During these early years I had been an occasional visitor to Abundant Life Church in Bradford. I had been very inspired by Paul Scanlon's teaching and by the culture of the church, and their vision to make the Gospel relevant to people in the 21st Century. I remember very vividly, for example, the time when Paul had talked about leaders freeing themselves from the attempt by some members of their congregation to contain and control them. He especially said that we leaders should free ourselves from the tyranny of people who threaten to leave unless we do as they wish. I think one of Paul's most profound observations about church life is that some people come and some people go. I remember being very motivated and returned home with a new attitude and a determination not to have my sleep disturbed again by worries about people leaving, or the games they play. Fascinatingly, within a short while my new resolve was tested. A member of the congregation demanded that something happen or she would leave. It was definitely not part of our plans so I said: 'that's not going to happen.' She said: 'well I will leave then.' I said: 'bye then.' She said quite aggressively: 'what did you say?' I said: 'Good bye and go with my blessing.' She looked at me for a moment, stunned, and then said: 'Oh, oh, well I am not leaving then.' This was a moment when I think I switched to a new view of church leadership and I have been free of that kind of control ever since.

My encounter with the refreshing new way that the guys at Abundant Life were doing church led me to take a long hard look at the way we did things. I realized that the style of our ministry and worship was in danger of becoming out of date. We had the feel of the 1980s, and society was definitely moving to a new place in this new millennium. We needed a fresh approach to communicating the Gospel to match the new building we were working on. We discussed this in our leadership team and decided to take a trip up to Bradford to observe their worship and see what we could learn. I hired a bus, and we made the journey one cold February afternoon in 2006. Our intention was never to become a clone of Abundant Life, but to see what principles we could learn from the way they did things and to pinch some good ideas (with their blessing!). We filled every one of the 52 seats with the entire leadership team, the Bridge Centre Board, the technical team, musicians, preachers and other team leaders. They took note pads and we learned a whole series of crucial lessons.

I think the first thing that struck us was the very **friendly welcome**. The car park stewards in their high-vis jackets smiled and waved us into place. I was personally greeted four times before I got to my seat in the auditorium. **Team work** was evident everywhere. In fact it is very clear that it is impossible to grow a numerically large church without a strong team ethos.

We were impressed by the **commitment to excellence** and high standards in everything. The place was polished clean, information leaflets were glossy, coffee was bean to cup quality, technical equipment was professional standard and the music was at a level you would expect to experience in a high quality rock concert. The worship was **culturally relevant**. All the old style churchy stuff which puts people off had been removed. The Gospel was the same, but it had been **dressed in new clothes**.

This had clearly had a dramatic effect on the demograph of the church, which was young. Even the older people seemed young at heart. I liked the **inclusive and compassionate culture** and the way that people from all walks of life were welcome. The style of leadership was very **informal and relational**, and differed markedly from the hierarchical style in evidence in many traditional churches. Informality is a feature of 21st Century life and the reason why many people find it difficult to connect with formal worship. They were clearly trying to make church a **fun place** to be. There was a lot of laughter, welcoming smiles, social activity, good music and engaging visual presentations. It felt like a place to which you would be **comfortable bringing** an unchurched friend, which, above all else, is the most significant point. Those of us in church tend to judge what goes on there by what we like and are used to. Then we wonder why nobody else comes. We need to look at things from the perspective of a friend or work colleague and think whether they would be able to engage with what we do and whether we would be comfortable inviting them anyway. This encounter with a new style of church is as significant in our journey as the decision to create the Bridge Centre.

So we decided to reinvent our church, putting into practice many of these things.

We decided our church would be a welcoming place where everyone was accepted and loved. We went for culturally relevant worship, ditching the old hymns and formality, and aiming for soft rock music and visual presentation of the highest quality. In fact we have tried to go for excellence in everything. We have dressed the old Gospel in new clothes, which we hope will persuade an unchurched person to stay long enough to connect with Jesus. I love to point out that we now have several examples of people who decided to join our church while still on the car park because the guy in the high-vis smiled and welcomed them. We made all these changes during the Summer of 2006 while we were in the thick of the refurbishment of the Bridge Centre as well. Were we crazy? Probably!

To symbolise this radical shift in the culture of our church we decided to change its name. So we are now called The Potter's House 21ˢᵗ Century Church. We used the name of our old community centre (which we had closed as the Bridge Centre project developed) because we wanted to emphasise three important ideas. Firstly, that **the church belongs to God**, it is His place. Secondly, the well known reference to the potter's house in Jeremiah 18 reminds us that He is the Potter and we are the clay and we have tried to make our House a place where **people can be moulded** into the likeness of Christ. Thirdly, because our city is known as 'The Potteries', this new name seemed appropriate, because we were in the process of becoming a **'drive to' City centre church** rather than one which just served the local Birches Head area.

We developed a church DNA which describes the characteristics of church we have tried to build:

- A large City church.
- The Lord's house, guided, inspired and filled with the Holy Spirit.
- A house of prayer.

- A centre for the development of media, arts and creativity.
- Young at heart.
- Friendly and welcoming.
- Having high standards in all its activities.
- Inclusive and compassionate.
- Culturally relevant in the style of its activities.
- Reaching the lost relationally.
- Resourcing, mentoring and training people so they can fulfil their potential.
- Working in partnership and unity with other members of the Body of Christ in Stoke-on-Trent.

The old ways of doing church are no longer reaching the people of the UK and I passionately believe that a new model of Christianity must arise (and thankfully is arising) in this land. It will be characterised by relevant ways of communicating the Gospel, using every modern technological means. It will be strongly connected to the community, sharing the love of Jesus in many practical ways. It will minister to people from cradle to grave. The people will be committed to friendship evangelism especially in the workplace. There will be new style leadership, which releases people's gifts and talents and is committed to a team approach. There will be a return to spiritual values like prayer, sin and salvation, the indwelling Holy Spirit and holiness. A spirit of excellence will pervade all. This new church will be dynamic, lively and fun to be in. It will grow by making many new disciples of Jesus Christ. It will dress the timeless truths of the Gospel in new clothes.

Chapter 17

Cultural language

The key question that any church leader must address is: how do I build a church that connects?

The reasons why most people do not go to church any more in this country are many and complex. However I do believe that the most significant barrier is cultural language. It is true to say that sixty or more years ago a majority of people were only one step away from becoming Christians; that of actually hearing the Gospel and making their personal response. In those days people encountered the Christian message much more readily than today, it was taught, for example, in schools, and a majority of children still went to Sunday school. They were, therefore, far more familiar with the language and culture of church than most people in Britain today. I believe that nowadays most people are two steps away from making a decision to follow Jesus; they still need to hear and think through the Gospel but the more formidable barrier they have to cross is that of understanding the culture of church. In traditional church we have a cultural language that most people today just cannot understand and do not wish to partake in.

Chocolate cake made with curry powder will always be revolting and never fit for purpose. The wrong ingredients, however carefully, sincerely and lovingly mixed will never produce a chocolate cake that is palatable. Good intentions are just not enough. To change the metaphor, if you go to the hospital with a broken arm you would not expect to be given an enema or barium meal. They are just not the right medicine for that particular problem. The sad truth is that traditional styles of church, however well intentioned, are not going to be more than a tiny minority interest activity in our present culture. We just do not speak the language that people can understand. Imagine that we invited the best Christian evangelist in the world, who preached the most persuasive message that has ever been preached in the history of the Church, but he spoke it in Swahili. No one would be moved, no one would decide to follow Jesus, because no one would have a clue what he was talking about.

Let me act like a doctor and give a diagnosis. The traditional denominations in this country are in serious difficulties. People have largely stopped going to church, in fact many are adopting a strongly atheistic position. Though there are some great, lively, full churches, they are not the norm. Traditional church will largely die out in the next 20 years unless there is change. The demographic profile of the traditional denominations is disastrous. We are failing to connect with the mind of most people today. We need a 21st (not 20th) century style which speaks the cultural language that the majority of people can understand. To give some examples of this:

- People expect hotel standard comfort, not hard pews, cold gloomy halls and dirty toilets.

- We live in a visual not audio world yet most of traditional services are audio only.
- People do not listen to organ music in the car on the way to work and find it unappealing. They struggle to understand the imagery of hymns and the language of 'thee' and 'thou' is quaint and rather weird to their ears.
- People are used to a 'weekend casual' style and find the stiff formality of 'Sunday best' not really to their taste.
- People are used to sound bites, and may find long sermons boring, especially if they contain words, stories or illustrations which do not relate to present day life.
- People expect to be warmly welcomed, and find it embarrassing to be ignored, or, if the talk from the front contains in-jokes to which they are not party.
- People are used to an increasingly informal society and much business is conducted relationally so they find church hierarchy and deference to authority hard to stomach.

We need to change all of this and more before we can even begin to engage people in a conversation about the Christian faith, which can seem rather hard to fathom for people who have been brought up in church, the culture of which seems normal and ordinary to them. Yet to people outside, church can seem like a foreign land. I have never been inside a betting shop in my life. If I went in one I would feel awkward and out of place. I would not have a clue what to do and I would have only a vague idea what the language of 'form' was really all about. That is how many unchurched people would feel if they came to a traditional church and, unless we Christians find ways to bridge that first barrier, they will not come.

When Hudson Taylor went to China in the late 1800s his mission was at first a failure until he started to dress as the native Chinese and talk their language. I believe Hugh Bourne would not be on Mow Cop but on the TV and internet if he were alive today. I think if he were around now, Charles Wesley would say: 'stop singing those old dirges I wrote before; get me some contemporary tunes and I'll write some stuff people can connect with'. It is a fascinating fact that after the fire and innovation of Wesley's revival, which took the Gospel to the masses in Britain, the Methodists soon slipped into a form of worship which became increasingly difficult for ordinary people to access. So when Hugh Bourne began his new movement in the early 1800s he rejected the Wesleyan style as being boring and out of date.

The church has just got to change.

Are we leading people into famine or abundance? Malawi and Zambia are side by side. One suffers from famine and lack, the other enjoys an abundance of food; the difference is how the land is farmed. We need to be wired up as pioneers, not maintainers. We need to abandon the old styles in favour of a radical new approach. Church has declined because of an old fashioned pride and a stubborn refusal to contemplate change. As the wind of change has blown across society many church people have turned their faces against it, refusing to budge on a style of worship that has long gone past its sell by date. Instead of engaging with the new culture around them, helping to shape the church to be relevant to it, and ensuring their church remains in it, they have tried to resist it. One by one, they are closing. It is a national tragedy; an emergency. Change is often cruel but the only way to survive it is to be part of it. Organs, stiff backed pews, KJV Bibles were all wonderful in their day, but those days are largely gone. We have to be like the revivalists of the 18th Century whose mission was to take the Gospel to the masses of the ordinary people. I see signs of hope where parish churches are becoming centres of village life once more and where new style churches are springing up in many towns and cities. Much more remains to be done, however.

In Luke 19v1-10 we have the vivid story of Jesus' encounter with Zacchaeus, the tax collector. The little guy up the tree was very unpopular with his peers because he collected for the hated occupying Romans and possibly because he was cheating them by collecting more than he should for his own gain. He was considered a 'sinner' with whom no respectable person would associate. Worse, the Jews believed that 'sin' could be passed from one person to another by simple contact so they would not even enter a 'sinners' house for fear of contamination which would require a ceremony of ritual cleansing before they could worship God again. So Zacchaeus was a reject. He was, in effect, outside the church, looking in curiously, but never able to enter. The way that Jesus dealt with Zacchaeus gives us some helpful insights into how we can build a 21st century church which connects.

The way Jesus helped Zacchaeus was to build a relationship with him first. Preaching at him or denouncing him publicly would not have saved him but only emphasized his sense of rejection and isolation. The pattern of traditional church in the West in the past has too often been: 'Behave...believe...belong'. Conformity to the norm was the expected pattern of behaviour throughout the early to mid 20th Century. All that changed in the Sixties. Nothing could be further from the truth now and in the 21st Century anything goes.

In 21st Century church we must turn this pattern on its head: 'Belong…believe…behave'.

So we welcome people and help them to feel loved and accepted first. Realising that sin is wrong comes out of a relationship with Jesus, not just by being told so (because the reaction will be…that's ok for you…but not for me) There is a delicate balance here which is not easy. To love and accept people, but encourage them to find Jesus and live better lives, is quite a difficult balance to achieve. In the end we cannot compromise on sin. Jesus did not, but His acceptance of Zacchaeus led to genuine repentance and a change of lifestyle.

The way we have tried to interpret this truth at The Potter's House is to emphasise friendship evangelism. We have a compact with the people. They will try to genuinely befriend, pray for, talk to, be kind to and eventually invite unchurched people to church events. We will try to put on worship and events which are 'cringe free' and which we think unchurched people can access.

Coffee is really important in this plan, as are food, fun and the arts (music, dance, drama, film, puppets etc). We try to offer a very warm welcome to everyone and to create a helpful supportive environment. Friendship not Bible bashing is the key to success. For example, we recently put on a comedy night. It was billed as clean comedy to which people could invite their friends as a first introduction to church. If one of the comedians had started to swear and tell filthy jokes it would have been a complete betrayal of trust (it was a very funny night and completely clean!). It is an illustration of how important it is to observe the covenant between the church and the people.

Jesus dealt with Zacchaeus's real issue – one of rejection – by inviting himself to tea, associating with him and risking defilement and rejection himself. 21st Century church must identify with people's real needs and try to meet them – by getting our hands dirty. We are His hands and feet now. We must try, in effect to, invite ourselves for tea, or get along side people, whatever their problems, issues or sinful behaviour.

In practice we have learnt that prayer is a really effective tool for evangelism. 21st century society has largely changed from even the recent past, and, where before people might have been embarrassed by the thought of prayer, now many will accept, even welcome prayer, especially for healing. People don't want to be told what to believe or to be preached at, but will welcome the love that accompanies prayer. Our observation is that a style of evangelism which offers something instead of invading people's space is becoming particularly effective.

Some people seem to think that as the population ages there will be more OAPs who will enjoy the more traditional forms of church, so our churches will naturally fill up and we must preserve our old style worship. It is a vain hope and nothing could be further from the truth. I am a baby boomer and I will not suddenly morph into my parents when I hit 65 and neither will most of my contemporaries. Our tastes, style preferences and cultural language are totally different to those of the previous generation. The '60s was a watershed. I prefer rock music. The organ is a hideous whining row to my ears. If you ask me why music is so important, you do not understand my generation. The truth is that most people of my generation will just not be comfortable in a traditional style service. We will not be there. We will not change as we get older. The church must find new ways to connect with the mind of my generation if they are ever to have a chance of explaining the Gospel to us. And these are only the baby boomers; even more change will be needed if we are to reach generations X and Y which are following.

Where the church does change and where it reaches out with the genuine Gospel message but dressed in new clothes it will find a ready audience and a new generation of disciples.

I include here a note which was recently left for us by a couple who visited our church and which illustrates the point about friendship:

Hi Phil,

I came this morning with my wife Diana and Lewis (my son) and his cousin Nathan. Me and Diana were impressed with the young lads doing car park duty, and the young lady doing greeting was fantastic to see. We felt really at home from then on. I felt a real gentleness about the building, My wife loved the first guy's story of emeralds, rubies and pearls. God had already shown her a picture to do with myself and these gems (God is very funny how he confirms). We loved the worship and Paul's talk. I loved what Paul said about getting our hands dirty. That's where my heart is. I love the community we call church but I love to be amongst the ones that don't know our Lord. After the service we stayed for a cup of tea and both me and Diana were impressed greatly that two of your welcome team, John and Sue, sorted us out and not only said 'hi' but were genuinely interested in finding a little out about us. And just when we thought we couldn't feel more at home as we were leaving you yourself interrupted your conversation with someone else to introduce yourself. Me and my wife Diana want you all to know at the POTTERS HOUSE STOKE-ON-TRENT that your church is friendliest church we have been to. Please pass on our love to all at your church.

May all Churches follow your great example thanks again may the King of kings bless your house.

Gaz & Diana.

Chapter 18

2C7

In September 2001 an Experian report had come out ranking Stoke 376 out of 376 in a range of socio-economic indicators. Our City was bottom of the pile. I was saddened by this statistic because I love my City and it seemed to me that the stigma of being considered the worst in the country would only increase the City's problems. My concern was shared by other Christian leaders, and so, influenced and supported by Saltbox Christian Centre (an ecumenical resource for churches in the area), we decided to hold a day conference on 31st October at Shallowford House, a local Anglican retreat centre, to reflect on the report and to pray. I think it is really important that we Christian leaders raise our heads from the work of building church and look around us. There is a wider body of Christ from which to draw strength and there is a city with which to engage. The world is much bigger than my little patch.

At the end of September there was an interdenominational gathering of Christians to watch the second 'Transformations' film at the George Hotel in Burslem. About 150 people showed up. At the end of the film, Lloyd Cooke, CEO of Saltbox, who had arranged the meeting, stood up and said: 'Do you want this?' A loud chorus of: 'Yes, yes' was the reply. Lloyd said: 'Then we need to pray' and on the spur of the moment he announced that there would be a unified prayer meeting on the evening of 31st October.

Twenty or so concerned leaders from across the denominations showed up at Shallowford on the morning of the 31st. As we talked together I was struck by the remarkable sense of unity and shared responsibility displayed by everyone in the room. The discussion during the day focussed not only on the problems of the City but also on the thought that the church was in an equally perilous state and was actually culpable to some extent in the way our City had declined over many years. Maybe it was time for repentance. We were reminded of a very significant picture which had been given during a previous interdenominational prayer breakfast in which the Lord said that we had experienced rain showers several times in recent years but because the ground was hard the water had run off, rather than soaking into the soil. He said that we should dig deeper to create a well in which to contain the water of His presence. The picture was of a deep quarry where hundreds of people were digging and toiling with tears of repentance, prayers and humility. This prophetic insight was to prove crucial in our understanding of what was to come.

During the final session we prayed for each other and the City, and then gathered in a circle and agreed to stand together in unity for the welfare of the City. We decided to lay aside historic differences and to work in cooperation, rather than competing with each other or being threatened by another's success. I have rarely experienced the manifest presence of God so powerfully as in that meeting.

That evening over 200 people showed up at the united prayer meeting. We asked various leaders to share some of their stories and to give their reflections on the challenges we faced in the City. One senior leader – Steve Russell – came forward and asked for forgiveness for any hurt or offence his church or denomination had caused. Lloyd invited other leaders to stand with him as a sign of forgiveness and unity. The meeting broke open as a wave of the Holy Spirit flooded in and people came weeping to the front kneeling in humility, repentance and reconciliation. We stayed a long time in God's presence praying for each other and for the City and it seemed to me that work on digging the well had begun. We announced that we would meet again in a month, on the last day of November.

On 30th November, 200 became 300, and we continued in the same vein: worshipping, praying, sharing and weeping in utter humility. Some people were worried that we were not 'praying' enough in the traditional sense but I think that we had stumbled on something new. It was all prayer.

At the end of December over 500 people turned up on a terribly frosty and snowy night. We took communion together. The meeting was marked by a deep level of repentance, humility and seeking God for mercy. We began to pray very creatively in groups, in pairs, from the front, in prayer lines and in song. We made use of visual aids and invited people to share their passion for the City and the work of God. What had begun as a hastily convened day conference for leaders to share their concerns for the City was rapidly developing into a prayer movement across the City. It was a God thing. The Holy Spirit gave us a verse which became our watchword, 2 Chronicles 7:14:

> '*If my people, who are called by my name, will humble themselves and pray and seek my face and turn from their wicked ways, then I will hear from heaven, and I will forgive their sin and will heal their land.*' (NIV)

We needed a name for our meetings which we took from this verse and 2C7 was born. Our meetings were led by Lloyd Cooke, and Robert Mountford, pastor, Bible college lecturer and director of City Vision Ministries. They were supported by a team of pastors, vicars, ministers and other Christian leaders from a variety of different denominations.

Over the next year we met monthly, and crowds of people came to pray and repent. I vividly remember the February meeting held in Longton Central Hall attended by over 700. The date coincided with the launch of Cross Rhythms City Radio who had been granted a five year local community licence and we did a count down to the first live broadcast from the prayer meeting. During the year two further key things happened to turn us to looking inside out.

A couple, Janet and Brian Street, who were trying to help street girls on a voluntary basis, asked for prayer. We had them share their story at the next meeting and we prayed for them and the girls. In response to the prayers their team began to grow. This led us to highlight other people who were working on voluntary caring initiatives in the City and more interdenominational teams started to develop.

Also we stumbled across the idea of engaging with and praying for different sectors of society. We invited key strategic leaders – police, fire, health, politics, education, social services etc – onto the stage to share about their work and concerns. Meeting by meeting we would pray for an area of civic life in turn. In 2002, for example, the City was debating whether or not to move to an elected mayoral system. We prayed for the whole issue and invited the candidates onto the stage to share their concerns for the City. I remember we hosted them in a small pre-meeting gathering in a side room, and one candidate nervously asked if this group was the prayer meeting, and what was that big group of people doing next door? We smiled and said: 'That's the meeting we are going into.' When we took them into the cauldron of 500 singing, dancing, worshipping Christians I think they were awestruck.

City issues – real issues – had come into the heart of prayer, and for seven years we held more or less monthly united, interdenominational prayer meetings. They were characterized by unity, humility, repentance, passionate prayer and the manifest presence of God. Our parting words were always: 'deeper much deeper' which I think encapsulated the spirit and intention of 2C7.

The 2C7 prayer movement spawned many other important things:

- A monthly City leaders meeting began, and has continued to meet. It is half a day of worship, prayer, fellowship, sharing and unity where strangers become friends and dividing walls are broken down.
- The Beacon house of prayer has been set up, led by William and Karen Porter and empowered by a wonderful group of prayer warriors. This has proved to be very strategic in terms of resource and prayer and is flourishing. At the time of writing they are aiming for 24/7 prayer coverage for the whole of 2012.

- We have added value to many social initiatives and opened the eyes of many Christians to the needs of vulnerable people.
- We developed periods of 24/7 prayer which have involved Christians across the North Staffordshire/South Cheshire region. This began with a week, then a month and lastly 40 days of prayer and fasting where churches and groups take a twenty four hour slot.
- We have encouraged local churches to develop their prayer life and pick up City themes using Jeremiah 29:7 and the inspiration:
  'Also, seek the peace and prosperity of the city to which I have carried you into exile. Pray to the LORD for it, because if it prospers, you too will prosper.' (NIV)
- We have held mission months. These happened because people pressed us to do some evangelism. Lloyd Cooke had a random encounter at a Methodist leader's house in Southampton with Craig Marsh who was an itinerant evangelist. Craig had an amazing testimony of his own healing from terminal cancer and had been travelling the world leading missions. So in September 2005 we invited Craig to lead a ten day mission to be held in a marquee at Trentham Gardens. Thousands attended, hundreds made first time decisions to follow Jesus, and even more came forward for prayers for healing. We called it 'A time for healing'. This was so fruitful we arranged a further four week mission in March 2006 which went on for ten weeks and which was held in four different locations around the City. It was an anointed time – Christians who had lost faith returned, people were converted and I still hear stories of

people who were miraculously healed. Hundreds of people spent hours standing, sitting, kneeling and lying down in the presence of God, which was a new phenomenon. People drawn from many churches across the region staffed the nightly meetings and provided teams for response, ministry, intercessors, stewards, security and worship.

- In 2010 we held the first civic prayer breakfast in the King's hall, Stoke (the City Hall). We invited the great and good of the City – the Lord Mayor, Councillors, MPs, the Chief Executive, Local Authority Officers, Police Chief, leaders of various key sectors like health, community leaders and church leaders from across the denominations. We produced a sheet of 'prayer goals' for the coming year and we prayed for the welfare of the City. It was very well received and the civic leaders, who, I believe, felt affirmed and supported, requested that it become an annual event.

I believe that the result of all these things has been to release the river of God in our City which Ezekiel 47 describes. We are probably still only ankle deep but I have a sense that the super tanker of social and spiritual decline is gradually being turned around. Many Christians complain about the state of the church and nation but I think the fault lies with us. We simply do not shine brightly enough. The issue is not the quality and quantity of the darkness but the quality and quantity of the light. If we want the work of God to prosper then we must pray.

Chapter 19

Gold

We laid down the 2C7 movement in October 2008 after exactly seven years. We believe the Holy Spirit told us to plant it in the ground as a seed, and then wait for the next stage of God's plan to germinate. In the later meetings we had started to focus on John 11:40 for our inspiration:

> 'Then Jesus said, "Did I not tell you that if you believe, you will see the glory of God?"' (NIV)

During Easter 2009 I was given a picture which I shared at a united leaders meeting. I saw the entrance to a mine of the sort you might see in a black and white picture from the American Wild West. A railway line led to the cave entrance; an empty rail car stood upon the rails around which stood miners armed with picks and shovels. The Lord said: 'You have spent seven years mining for silver which has blessed and prospered the city; now you will mine for gold. But gold is mined differently than silver.' In September of that year I was at the Stronger Conference at Abundant Life Church when I received a text from my good friend Jon Bellamy, CEO of Cross Rhythms. In it he said that gold had been discovered in Staffordshire - what an amazing God-incidence! It was the first news of the beautiful Anglo Saxon hoard of gold which had been unearthed in a field in mid-Staffordshire. Amongst all the finely wrought items was a gold strip which carries the Latin inscription: *'Rise up O Lord, and may thy enemies be dispersed and those who hate thee be driven from thy face.'* It has two sources: the Book of Numbers or Psalm 67, taken from the Vulgate, the Bible used by the Saxons. I believe it is a message to us from God which He had hidden in the ground over a thousand years ago and which suggests that we are on the edge of unearthing the gold of God's glory. Will it be a tsunami or a rising tide? We wait to see.

What is the glory? It is, of course, the manifest presence of God. But how is that felt and expressed? How is it outworked? It is definitely not a self indulgent Christian 'bless me' party. I have come to believe that at least part of the meaning of the parable of the gold is that it represents people wrestled from the darkness of their separation from God, brought into the light, taken through the refiner's fire and made into the purest vessels of grace. Being at heart an evangelist I would take this view, of course, but there is no denying that an increase in the number of people finding salvation would increase God's glory on the earth. If the glory is an increase in the manifest presence of God, then that must be outworked in greatly increased Holy living, enthusiasm, healing, wholeness and salvation. It must surely cause the Kingdom to grow and society to be transformed.

So we wait for the seed to germinate with hope, expectation and prayer.

This continuing prayer movement has had a profound effect upon the life of The Potter's House. Prayer is a priority for us. Indeed,

134

I believe that, without much prayer of all sorts, our efforts to extend God's Kingdom will largely be in vain. You cannot build the Kingdom without the sort of passionate, persistent prayer which moves God's heart. So, besides resourcing and encouraging private prayer, we regularly meet corporately for prayer. Most notable of these meetings have been the Arise events which developed after the monthly 2C7 meetings ended. I am of the opinion that the Holy Spirit intended 2C7 to find its next expression in the local church. Well over 100 of us meet once a month on a Sunday evening for an event which is guided entirely by the Holy Spirit. Though the Spirit tends to give us in advance a theme for each evening, we have no other agenda or plan. We worship and pray in a style which is similar to the 2C7 meetings, and is characterized by passion, variety, creativity and spontaneity. The presence of God is heavily upon us as we seek His face. We have seen many answers to our prayers and several dramatic healings. In the spring of 2011, as I write this book, there has been a development in the Arise meetings. Before our April meeting the Holy Spirit told us to have no theme, but to let the glory of God arise in the people. We discovered a new level of openness, freedom and the presence of God. Where these meetings will lead I do not know, though some are saying if we continue the Glory of God will be revealed. Maybe we are digging our own little vein of gold. Perhaps each person healed and restored, each person saved and each prodigal returned is like a little nugget of gold. We pray: 'more Lord, give us more.'

I include here a personal testimony by Rebecca Eagles to illustrate how prayer can change a life and which is also a parable for us in the City, that as we wait for the 2C7 seed to germinate, we must not give up (Galatians 6:9):

> In April 2010, I started to feel unwell. I had really low energy and suffered from headaches and dizziness. I went to the doctor, and blood tests showed that my blood sugar levels were very low. After this I was referred to see a specialist in endocrinology, and later a neurologist.

> Waiting for hospital appointments was frustrating, because I was feeling worse every day. Even hospital appointments seemed useless, as any tests that were done came back clear.

> The illness impacted heavily on my life, as I couldn't live my life in the way I wanted to. I struggled to even get to college, because by the time I got there I had already used up the little energy that I did have and I couldn't physically carry on. It also had a big impact on my family and close friends, as it was difficult to communicate how being ill was affecting me as it wasn't a physical or obvious illness. Also, I wasn't the lively upbeat person that they have always known me as so it was difficult for those around me to cope with my general lack of energy.

> During the time that I was ill, I had a lot of prayer at meetings like Arise. It was very encouraging to know that there were people who were praying for me throughout the illness, but it was also very hard because any amount of prayer didn't seem to be helping how unwell I was feeling.

In October 2010, I was still going to hospital for appointments and various tests, and still any tests were coming back as clear and the doctors had no real idea of how to treat me. I was almost at the point where I felt like giving up. I was beginning to think that maybe I was meant to just cope with it and live my life around the dizziness, headaches and low energy. Towards the end of October, I went away with the youth group for a few days to Dunfield House. During the holiday I was still considering whether I was supposed to just manage the illness, and thinking that I was meant to live with it. The theme of the meetings on the holiday was: 'We are alive'. I didn't feel very 'alive' at that point, I felt like I couldn't get on with my life and achieve the things I wanted to because I was being held back by the illness.

I was prayed for by a few of my closest friends at Dunfield house, and during this time of prayer I felt like the illness was lifted away from me, and my energy flooded back to me. As I was worshipping and praying a verse came to me, Isaiah 40:31 which says, 'But those who trust in the Lord will find new strength. They will soar high on wings like eagles. They will run and not grow weary. They will walk and not faint.' (NIV) It was then that I knew that God had healed me.

Ever since, I have been full of energy and back to my normal self.

Chapter 20

Refit

The raucous sounds of banging hammers and rasping saws echoed through the long empty corridors. The rhythmic sounds were occasionally punctuated by a crash, accompanied by cheers as the latest stubborn piece of partition wall or old central heating piping finally surrendered. As I wandered through the building in those early months of 2006 I would come across little groups of dust covered people hammering, smashing, yanking and dragging piles of rubbish to collecting points ready to be loaded into skips. Night after night, weekend after weekend, the people of the church crawled over the building like ants. Heroes all. We estimate that they put in £250,000 worth of voluntary work calculated at minimum wage.

I am reminded of the story in 1 Samuel 22 where David hid in the cave of Adullam with his little band of followers, many of whom were in some kind of distress. It seemed to be a commentary on the first dozen or so years of our journey as a church. However, David's story moves on because in 2 Samuel we have the description of how David moved from Adullam to Hebron and was joined by his mighty men. 1 Chronicles 12:23-38 lists these men and says that they understood the times they were in and came to Hebron fully determined to make David King over all Israel.

Our church people were like this and they set about the task of creating the Bridge Centre like David's determined warriors.

It took us many months just to strip out all of the old rubbish, fixtures and fittings left by the school and which either we did not want or needed to be replaced. We filled dozens – I lost count – of industrial sized, 'roll on roll off' skips during Saturday morning work parties. I vividly remember the struggle we had to pull up all the old carpet which had been firmly glued down and the revolting task of stripping out the pupils' toilets ready for a complete refit. Two guys, Keith Nixon and Roy Emery, took it upon themselves to remove the old coal fired boilers. These were enormous, screw fed machines slightly reminiscent of the boilers in the Titanic. They spent many evenings down in the dark boiler room covered in black coal dust, gradually cutting their way through the maze of huge iron pipes. They showed amazing resilience and persistence, which typified the spirit shown by so many people.

We became so focussed on the task that inevitably the regular activities of church life suffered, though to some extent this was balanced by the friendships which were forged and strengthened as we worked together. Church attendance did plateau for a while but we knew that, once the Bridge Centre opened, a whole new world of evangelical opportunity would open up for us.

Besides all the smashing and banging we also began to refurbish the building in the early months of 2006. Much of this work was completed by contractors but some was done using the skills of the people. For example, they did most of the joinery and decorating. One guy, Matthew Eagles, laid all the carpet by himself and a team planned and laid approximately ten kilometers of network cables. By March the security fencing had been erected around the perimeter which was a source of relief to us all and which largely curtailed the destructive vandalism that had plagued the site. We also saw work begin on the brick laying, road building, trench digging, plumbing, electrics, plastering, roofing, double glazed windows, partition walls, air conditioning, joinery, network cabling, lift installation, security systems, wiring and decorating. My biggest disappointment was that in the summer I missed the installation of the lift because I was on holiday. I know I probably sound like a complete nerd but the project was important to us and all I have got are pictures of the day when the huge crane arrived and hoisted the steel lift assembly completely over the building. I missed all the fun that day!

By the early months of 2007 a large portion of the refit work had been completed. We had welcomed our first tenants, and had appointed staff to oversee and manage the day to day operation of the site. We only had £650,000 to spend on the whole refit which we somehow managed to stretch to pay for all the most essential work. We had to curtail some of our grander schemes and some parts we did not finish until several years later. However, we did manage to get the building habitable and open for business. I think the church experienced a kind of 'project fatigue' at this time which is understandable considering the sacrifices that had been made in time, effort and money, so we called a halt to all voluntary building work for a long time. It has been worth it though, because we have created an amazing place.

The Bridge Centre Trust is an independent charitable trust company which owns runs and maintains the building and site. It employs a staff of five and is open seven days a week 7am till 10pm Monday to Friday and 8am to 3pm at the weekends (plus evenings when there is an event). It has 30,000 square feet of accommodation divided roughly into two halves. The two upper floors provide enterprise space for start up businesses and charitable groups and comprise approximately 30 units of varying sizes. I say approximately because some partition walls can be added or removed to suit the needs of clients. The ground floor is the public space and has two large halls, a conference suite, a coffee bar, a prayer room, offices and seven meeting rooms. It is set in 3.5 acres of grounds with 130 car parking spaces. It has the feel of a conference facility rather than a church and we have fitted it out with the sort of electronic equipment needed to service 21st century clients.

The Bridge Centre has become an incredibly vibrant place where on any given day there will be a mix of business, community and church activities taking place as is illustrated here by the following account of a day in the life of the Bridge:

Tuesday

7am   John Phillips, one of the duty managers arrives.
7:20am   the nursery staff arrive.
7:30am   the doors open and the first parents arrive to drop children off at the nursery.
         The domestic staff arrive and begin cleaning and preparing rooms and setting up the catering for the day.

8:00am   Conference leaders start to arrive to set up and people arrive to begin work in the businesses upstairs (approximately 30 people at the time of writing).

8:30am   Kath Allen, the other duty manager arrives along with conference delegates. The first refreshments are served.

9:00am   Conferences begin. In the main auditorium there are
till   100 people attending a PCT training event. In the
12:30pm   community rooms there are meetings for Crossroads, Pertemps, Kier and a group from Newcastle College doing drama for disabled young people. (15-25 in each group)

In the prayer room a church group is meeting to pray, church staff are busy in the offices, and Little Bridges, the church's parent and toddler group is in full swing (25 children plus parents).

During the morning people are popping in and out to the Police Post upstairs and clients are coming to Family Support Services for counselling.

12:30pm   Lunch is served for various groups in the coffee lounge

1:30pm   Some of the conferences continue through the afternoon.

4:00pm   The atmosphere begins to change as all those people gradually leave and the City Music School staff start to prepare the rooms for the children.

4:30pm   Approximately 150 children occupy most of the rooms and the sound of music fills the whole building.

7:30pm   The mood changes again as the children leave and people begin arriving for the evening activities. There is a Bible study, a dance class, an art class, a Children's Services training group, a District Labour Party meeting, and a Street Pastor's training meeting.

10:00pm The building closes, before which, the domestic staff complete a cleaning cycle and some rooms are prepared for the next day.

The following day would see a completely different collection of conferences and groups using the building. Some days are quieter than this; sometimes every room in the building is in use. Some of the rooms can be used four times a day with a brief, hectic changeover between groups. This can sometimes create tension as different groups learn to work in a shared space and church people have to demonstrate plenty of humility as they share their own building with others, but that is what the Gospel is all about. Our mandate from the Lord was to create a place where the church and the world could mix up together. This we have achieved, and it is a real joy to walk the corridors of the Bridge and see such a wide variety of good work going on. I am also very glad that people have found their way into the life of the church through attending a secular event at the Bridge; there are even some who have found faith for the first time and who have come from completely non-church backgrounds.

The Bridge Centre was worth all the effort. Apart from providing us with a home we have enriched the community life of Birches Head, invested in the economic growth of the City and most important of all, made Jesus more accessible to people.

Chapter 21

Leadership

I am not going to attempt to unpack the issue of leadership to any great depth, but merely include here a few points which I consider absolutely essential to successful church leadership.

Leading church has been quite creatively described as trying to walk up a down escalator. Standing still and trying to maintain the status quo by holding on to what you have got will inevitably see decline as a congregation ages. The only way to grow church is to take imaginative and energetic leaps up the demographic time bomb by trying to make new disciples of Jesus Christ and that takes real leadership.

Leadership matters…it really does.

It is quite surprising to analyse what causes churches to grow. Not what might be expected, as for example, by a 'move of the Spirit', which many are always waiting for. They are 'waiting for godo' in my opinion. Some people have been saying that a revival is just about to come since the 1970s…always waiting, never acting. In that time the church has generally suffered a catastrophic decline in the UK. In surveys of growing churches the consistently significant factor was strong leadership.

What is strong leadership?

Leadership is not the same as management. Management is defined as:

> 'The skilful handling or use of something such as resources; the organizing and controlling of the affairs of a business or a sector of a business.'

Management is controlling what is already there; deploying existing resources; maintaining.

Real leadership is about vision, driving things forward, making changes, empowering others, developing and creating. Leadership is always on the edge. Management stays in the box; real leadership asks 'what box?' Of course every true leader has to engage in some management. The key issue is where the balance lies.

I think there is sometimes a fault with the way Christian leaders are formed and trained. They often appear to be chosen for their management ability, usually their pastoral skills, and so by instinct they try to shepherd the flock, to maintain. This can lead to the unintentional creation of a maintenance mode of ministry which inevitably ages and declines. I believe this is the most significant reason for the disaster which has befallen the church in the UK in the latter half of the 20th Century.

And, of course, **true leaders have followers.** Leadership is not about 'me', by which I mean it is not about 'me' finding 'my' identity in leading by feeling a sense of importance or power. No, our identity should be found in Christ Jesus. However, I have observed that too many so called leaders in both the church and secular worlds make this mistake. They exhibit behaviour which suggests they feel threatened by the gifts and talents of others and they try to be one man bands. It puzzles me why so many leaders behave like this because one man band growth is limited to your capacity to cope...it will be small. Small minded equals small numbers because we are not omni-competent and we need teams to help us. It is virtually impossible to give pastoral care personally to more than 100 people, for example, and for most leaders it will be a much smaller number than this. It is a trap we must try to avoid as leaders if we want to see God's Kingdom penetrate deeply and widely into the society around us.

I have tried to model a different kind of leadership by concentrating on empowering and releasing others to do the work and by developing a strong team ethos. I will share a couple of examples of this:

Firstly, as I have previously indicated, though I lead a church I am involved in very little pastoral work. This is not because I am uncaring, nor are the people at the Potter's House left without support. Instead I have **a team of people far more gifted than me** who do all the pastoral visiting and counselling that is required. I am merely a member of that team and they deploy me occasionally when they think my particular skills will be useful. There can be an unspoken pressure for the vicar to visit and some church leaders seem to spend a huge amount of their time whizzing round on an endless visitation programme. Why? Let someone else do it. Creating a visiting team makes use of people's gifts and leaves the leader free to do other things such as to plan and strategise and put energy into pushing for growth.

Secondly, though I am the senior leader and could choose to preach most Sundays, I forego this choice in favour of a team approach. So I will only preach once a month, the rest of the appointments being **taken by a team of preachers** supplemented by the occasional visitor. This has many advantages. It means that I am released from the constant pressure of writing sermons on a weekly basis, which frees me to do other things. Also this helps my preaching to be fresh because I have had time to think about it. It also brings variety into the preaching because each member of the team has their own unique approach. Of course, we do take care to ensure that the preachers on our team are theologically sound and preach in a style that suits the ethos of 21st Century church. The people need and deserve an excellent diet of spiritual food, and their welfare must take priority above all other considerations.

The hoover can't say to the boiler, 'I am not like you so I am no use.' Both are needed for the efficient running of the house. In other words, **teams are king**. Occasionally visitors say to us: 'Aren't you lucky to have all these talented people doing all this work in your church?' Our answer is always that luck plays no part at all. The teams exist because we have intentionally built them. We have trained, empowered and released people into roles where they are flourishing and contributing. Any church can be like this if the leader sets about creating a culture of team work and actually releases authority to others. The parable of talents is very instructive here because the guy who hid his talent had it taken from him and it was given to the one who was using his existing talents most successfully. We can learn from this that, where we do create the right environment, we will attract gifted people who see an opportunity to serve, and our pool of talent will grow seemingly by miraculous means. We planted our church with only 17 adults and their children, which is a much smaller number than the average church in the UK, so there must be hope for every church to grow if the right strategy is employed.

At the Potter's House our whole church is organised into clusters of teams. I am the leader so I oversee the whole structure, but I do not get personally involved in much day to day work. We have a church leadership team which meets monthly which I chair, and most of these guys have an area of responsibility to lead and have their own teams.

I think the secret of growing a great church is to be the sort of leader who not only knows what needs to be done, but who has the skill to motivate others to do it. I believe the true gift of leadership is to be able to easily persuade people to do things. A leader will instinctively know how to create and motivate teams rather than always wanting to handle things themselves.

Perhaps it is time for some leaders to take a fresh look at the way they do things in the church.

Chapter 22

Vision

Leaders are vision casters and in this chapter I want to look at the necessity of communicating a vision and creating a consensus and ownership among God's people to see the vision realized.

A true leader lives part of his or her thought life in the future and is always thinking, planning, imagining, and constructing the future. A true leader is not satisfied with the status quo but gets frustrated, even angry if things stay the same. A true leader wants to encourage **change**, which is a very dirty word in many church circles because they have been inflicted by poor leadership for decades. A visionary leader is constantly communicating 'where we are going'. True leaders are able to persuade people to change, to come on the journey with them and to adventure into the unknown. The church is supposed to be a movement not a monument, and our task as leaders is to discern where the Holy Spirit wants to take us next. To be honest if you haven't got a vision, you are not a leader, because a leader will always be a keeper of the vision for the organization he or she leads.

Vision therefore is key to leadership and fundamental to us developing churches which remain relevant to each new generation. The vision must be relevant if we want people to follow it. For example a leader who casts a vision for us all to go back to living in caves is not going to attract many followers because that is leading us to the past not the future.

How do we discern God's will for a church?

The underlying vision for Christians is always going to be:

'Therefore, go and make disciples…' (Matt 28:19-20 NIV)

I understand from this that our vision is to make disciples, not converts. A disciple is a learner, a person who has absorbed the truth and grown to maturity. So that is our underlying mandate, not just to be nice to people or just do social work, but to make disciples of Jesus Christ. However, there will always be a specific vision for each church or organization which is based around our particular purpose and mandate from God, and it is the leader's role to discern, keep, build and communicate that vision.

The Bible makes it very clear what will happen if the leader does not do this. The well known verse from Proverbs 29:18 says:

*'Where there is no vision, **the people perish.'** (AV)

How do they perish? The NIV gives a slightly different translation which is illuminating: *'Where there is no revelation the people cast off restraint.'* This suggests to me that people run wild, go their own way and get lost in the wilderness when there is no revelation from God about the right direction to go in. So we learn from this that God provides the vision by His revelation.

The Holy Spirit will eagerly provide vision to Christian leaders who seek Him. In Jeremiah 29:11 God says: *'I know the plans I have for you.'* (NIV) The issue is whether leaders are prepared to be constantly seeking for vision from the Holy Spirit. It requires a huge and constant effort. If leading church is like trying to go up a down escalator then part of the challenge is constantly to take intuitive leaps forward into the Holy Spirit's purpose for our corporate life together. To stand still is inevitably to slide back into decline, as, first the movers and shakers, then the young people, leave in disappointment and disillusionment.

What is a vision?

It is simply a statement of where the leader sees things going. It gives direction and purpose. It is a straightforward statement of what we are trying to achieve or where we think the Holy Spirit is leading us and what He is asking us to do next.

In Luke chapter 10 we have the account of Jesus preparing and sending 72 of His followers out in twos. He cast a very clear vision of their purpose (to proclaim the Kingdom of God) and outlined the methods they were to employ (bringing peace, healing the sick etc). I learn from this that the aim of casting a vision is to **create a sense of momentum, adventure and direction**. People are motivated (especially men) by risk, challenge and adventure which the 72 certainly faced as they went forth.

It is crucial to understand that, though a vision may be synthesized into a clearly worded statement, it becomes a lifestyle, a distinctive DNA which is appropriate to the setting. So, for example, evangelism is not an event but a lifestyle, which is what Jesus was trying to build into His followers. Having said this, I think it is very helpful to publish a clearly worded document which outlines the way forward, and may be structured as follows:

Mission statement – sets out the main purpose of a church or group.

Vision statement – sets out how in a certain time frame we will continue to fulfil that purpose.

Plan – sets out how we as an organization will practically achieve our aims.

This sort of document will always:

> Build on the past. Look to the future. Have achievable goals. Be specific. Be easily grasped by people.

The challenge for the leader is then to communicate this vision frequently, and encourage the people to absorb it, so it is not just a written statement, but becomes a life style which is exemplified by the leader and lived out by the people.

At the Potter's House our mission statement has been formed around the Great Commission:

> To lead all people to become committed followers of Jesus Christ within a loving community of growing Christians.

Our vision has been to take people though a journey towards Christian maturity and is set out as follows:

A bringing people
We seek to win people for Jesus
Everyone is a missionary
A belonging people
We seek to encourage Christian friendship and belonging
Everyone is called to care in the name of Jesus
A maturing people
We seek to help people become true Christian disciples
Everyone is called to be holy
An enabling people
We seek to empower people to discover and use their gifts and talents
Everyone is in ministry

How do we build a vision?

- By listening to the Holy Spirit because He will whisper to us.
- By listening to people and allowing their input in the vision.
- By process. This will involve frequent review, reflection, discussion and synthesis (a new unified whole resulting from the combination of different ideas, influences, or objects).

The leader's role is to initiate the process and then keep the pot boiling year by year.

If a vision is always a continuing process, it cannot simply be imposed by a leader. To say: 'Here is the vision I am giving you, like it or lump it' is overbearing. It creates rebellion or passivity and is a form of bullying. It is evidence of weak leadership which feels threatened by the skills and strength of others. Vision must carry consensus and ownership of the people.

155

How do we communicate a vision?

- By influencing others through relationships with them. By winning them over.
- By being winsome in the way we persuade people.
- By creating ownership. Telling and owning are totally different.

The key is communicating effectively, regularly, pithily, clearly using every means at our disposal. At the Potter's House we use many different forms of media to communicate our vision such as: film, web, pictures and posters, printed word and aurally. We try to be as professional as we can, avoiding, for example, notice boards which are out of date and poorly presented. We try to inspire our people by using words like adventure, risk and challenge. In particular, Christians will always get inspired when we are aiming to help people find faith in Jesus.

In my experience if the vision is sensible, realistic and achievable they will go with it and a successful vision will come out of a consultative process and will create ownership, agreement, excitement and engagement.

Over the last 20 years we have worked hard to communicate the vision the Lord has laid on our hearts, and I believe it is one of the main reasons we have seen consistent growth every year except the one when we were in the thick of refitting the Bridge Centre premises.

Chapter 23

Two services

Building the Kingdom is like being on a continuing adventure, or maybe like being on a roller coaster where you never get off. It is a life full of surprises, thrills and challenges, one of the biggest of which is to maintain the momentum. Towards the end of 2007 it became increasingly evident that we were running out of seats on Sunday morning. The growth in attendance was fuelled by the increasing opportunities we were enjoying as the Bridge Centre opened up. It is great to have such a problem but the issue is that if it is not addressed then growth could be stifled. The accepted wisdom about church growth is that once a hall is over 80% full it is very difficult to grow any more. I guess the reason for this is that when 80% of the seats are full it actually seems as if there is no space left. This makes it difficult for new people to feel at home, because it appears cramped or intimidating, or maybe families can't sit together. Our auditorium had been at least 80% full every week, with the exception of one week at the beginning of the summer holidays; sometimes it was over 90% full. Therefore this was an issue that we had to address or we could lose all the momentum we had gained by our effort to create the Bridge Centre.

Change is probably one of the most challenging issues for people to face, so we had to approach the issue of creating more space with a lot of careful thought and planning. We began the process by devoting a whole senior leadership team meeting to discuss our options which we perceived were as follows:

- Move the whole church to a different, larger location. This was out of the question because we had only just laid down our tools from the Bridge refit, and we had neither the energy nor the money to begin another project so soon.
- Build a new and larger auditorium. This is a great option, but even if we had started immediately it would take three years at least to complete such a project, and the need was immediate.
- Plant a new church. This seems an obvious solution, as we are experienced in this field. However we felt the time was not right and that God wanted us to build a numerically larger church.
- Put on a second act of worship. It was clear that this was the only viable option, so discussion then centred round when to hold such a service.

After much debate we finally plumped for the following solution, and a communiqué outlining the practical arrangements was circulated to all the leaders as follows:

Due to significant increase in the number of worshippers over the last 18 months, below is a proposal for a new structure of worship at The Potter's House.

First service: 9:30 – 10:45am
Refreshments: 10:45 – 11:15am
Second service: 11:15am – 12:30pm

· The message and content of each service are to be exactly the same. Should added ministry time be needed after the first service, this will move into the prayer chapel.

· The same band will be required for both services, turning up at 8:45am for a sound check, not another practice. Practice remains on a Thursday evening.

· The Lighthouse (children's work) will operate at only one service with the exception of the crèche, which would potentially be needed for both. It has been advised that the best time for the Lighthouse to operate would be the 11:15am service.

· Two morning services is a quicker solution to an immediate need. Those taking part are required for up to an hour longer than they are currently. An afternoon, evening or midweek service means creating a whole new team to serve. We are currently lacking in some areas and need to strengthen what we have. Therefore, creating a whole new team is near impossible.

· There is a window for refreshments in the middle of the two services enabling people from both services to come together – those arriving and those departing.

As a leadership team, we believe this is the right direction to head in. It will undoubtedly have teething problems but we will make it work. There are issues to resolve and most importantly a strategy will need to be created with a view to how we inform and, most importantly, encourage everybody.

There will be concerns and obstacles whatever we choose. The important decision is not necessarily whether or not this is a perfect model to go by but rather can we make a decision soon before we lose momentum?

The next important move was to explain this to the congregation in order to persuade them to come with us on the journey. People need lots of reasons to be persuaded to accept change and so we gave them lots! I include here the full text of what we said to them:

- A missioning church does not mission if it is full. There is no point in us asking you bring friends if there are no seats for them. We need more seats. This is an issue we cannot ignore any longer.
- God has clearly told us to grow and change; to move on. You may remember that both Rob Phillips (preaching team) and Bishop Eddie Mulenga (visiting preacher) told us there would be change this year. God is doing a new thing. Here it is!
- The statistical evidence from church growth experts is that when a church gets above 80% full it usually does not grow much more. This is probably because people feel that there is not room for them, or they are uncomfortable, or they feel insignificant in a room that seems to be bursting at the seams, or they cannot sit together. We have been over 80% full for many months. This decision will create more seats. It will create growing room.
- Our church does not exist for its own sake, but for the world. Our purpose is to grow the Kingdom of God. We all agree that is it so nice and comfortable here but a sacrifice must be made for the sake of the lost.

- We are mature enough and blessed with enough resources and wonderfully skilled people to successfully make this next big step.
- We have always been a pioneer congregation. This change is not a one off but only the next step in the adventure. It is similar to when we moved from the conference room to this auditorium and the congregation grew. This step is a natural progression in the adventure.
- We want to create an environment where people can grow, contribute and be significant and this decision will create many more opportunities for people to get involved and use their gifts
- There are 240,000 reasons (the population of Stoke-on-Trent) out there why we should do this! We must create extra seats for people to hear the Gospel.
- We are in the most dangerous place for a church to be in. Everything is good; the hall is commodious and full of people. If we allow self satisfaction to set in, which is the precursor of pride, we will be sowing the seeds of stagnation and eventual decline. We must avoid falling into the maintenance ministry trap at all costs.
- We know that change is difficult and unsettling. We are asking you to be bold, to choose to wholeheartedly support this change for the sake of the Gospel. We think it is a change which will do us good.
- We know that you all really desire your friends and relatives to know Jesus. We know how much prayer and effort you are putting in. This is our response to that desire and it is an opportunity which we hope you will seize.

- You have come this far on the journey with us. Don't stop! Take the next step of the adventure. We hope you will support this decision and get excited about being a church that wants to grow. We hope it will spur us all on to tell our friends about Jesus. We believe it will create the space for new friends to come and discover a relationship with Him for themselves.

This presentation was well received by the whole congregation. The teams were trained, the stage was set and on March 1st 2008 we held two services. It went virtually without a hitch. In the years that followed we have seen the fastest period of growth in the short history of our church. We have proved the point, that when God asks us to build a bigger barn, he will fill it. At the time of writing our first service has grown to about half full, the second is hovering at the 80% full level and we are beginning to think again about what to do next to create more space.

Chapter 24

Timothy

It was during a summer holiday in 2006 at St George's House, Georgham, North Devon that I dropped a bombshell. A group of thirty or so people mainly in their twenties sat around the edge of the common room and listened to my talk about the future of the church. They had organised a holiday cum retreat for their age group to this Christian outdoor pursuit centre and had invited me to speak at one of their evening gatherings. What I released to them was a passion and conviction that had been growing in me during the preceding twelve months. I had decided that the time had come to be intentional about empowering and releasing them into senior leadership. I told them that it was my intention to hand over the church to them during the following years so that by their early thirties they would be running the show. I told them very plainly to get ready!

I have since come to call this age group the 'Timothy' generation, after the letters that St Paul wrote to his young protégé Timothy who quite clearly was being prepared to take over the leadership of the church in Ephesus that Paul had originally planted. In the years since my statement of intent, we have been very deliberately mentoring, training and releasing the people of their generation into leadership roles. It is a fundamentally important part of leadership to grow others as leaders so that the work can continue to prosper long after they have moved on. I actually believe leadership is best expressed through resourcing, empowering and releasing **others.** It is about empowering, not controlling, people. I am always grieved to see very able leaders who fail to do this, and, when they depart, everything they have built collapses.

In fact I have come to believe that **a leader's best work should take place after they have retired from leadership.** This may seem to be an extreme view but I believe that truly effective leadership is about what you have built in the people around you, how you have strengthened, trained, equipped, resourced and released them so they go on to do even greater exploits for the Lord than you. It is about **legacy**.

The Timothy generation at the Potter's House have taken their responsibilities very seriously and, at the time of writing, they are already fully responsible for many of the departments in the church. They are a group considered to be a 'missing generation' in national church life but not so in our church because we have given them a hope and a future; they have a purpose and a role and so they have stayed.

A key part of the strategy was to find a younger person to be my personal 'Timothy'; someone to whom we could confidently pass the burden of leadership when my time came to move aside. With this in mind I began to pray and ask God to show me who He had in mind for this role. In the end we chose a guy in his mid twenties called Paul Nixon. He had been converted through the ministry of the church, had grown strong in the Lord and had been leading our youth ministry for a number of years. I remember that I gave him an eye popping moment when I privately approached him to sound out whether he would be interested in taking a five year Associate Pastor position with a view to the possibility of taking over the senior role from me. He claims to have spent much time fasting and praying over the offer, but I know the truth – he wanted to bite my hand off!

In the summer of 2008 we appointed Paul as Associate Pastor and he began a process of learning on the job from me, and we also paid for him to receive much training, including taking a Master's Degree in Leadership, Renewal and Mission. I think Paul has proved to be an inspired choice. He has outstanding leadership gifts which everybody in our church recognizes.

He writes about his experience:

> During my time as the associate pastor, I have often found myself feeling one of two emotions. Firstly, I have felt worried that I am not up to the task of becoming the senior leader. Secondly, I have felt confident to take on the position immediately! So often have my feelings changed as each day has gone by that I have learned the valuable lesson of not letting my feelings dictate. The training period I have been through – including both practical and theoretical challenges – has been very important. It would be tempting to suggest that the transition of church leadership could take place within 12 months providing both individuals are agreed on the idea. I would disagree. The

time spent sharing, discussing and exploring the many areas of church leadership have been priceless. There have been times when the senior pastor and I have agreed and times when we have disagreed. Nevertheless, the end decision on a matter was not always of great importance. The importance lay in the journey we have travelled together.

From my point of view, the most valuable aspect of ensuring a smooth transition of leadership has been my relationship with the senior pastor. Over the past three years, he and I have discussed a whole host of subjects, issues and challenges without ever labelling it 'a meeting'. We have talked in person, on the phone and through email. His office, his phone and his home have always been open to me. Our conversations have formed part of a friendship that is full of mutual understanding and support. We look out for one another and take interest in each other's lives, rather than simply aiming to accomplish a task. I have felt valued, equipped and enabled without ever feeling 'second best' or 'not quite there' whether I was wrong or right. Without any doubt, this has been essential to my personal development and to stabilising the future leadership of the church.

In the summer of 2010 I began to think through the issue of when to hand over the leadership to Paul. I think about 98% of me knew that the time was fast approaching; a little bit of me wrestled with the decision for a while because the Potter's House has been my life's work, my calling, and letting go is sad in a way. However it is absolutely vital actually to do that which you have promised to do, so, after careful discussion with the senior leadership team, we decided that the time was right, and we announced to the church in November 2010 that I would be stepping aside from the role of Senior Pastor in the summer of 2012. I am not retiring but staying on to provide further support and mentoring to Paul. Again the decision has been met with universal agreement because everyone can see that he is the right man for the job.

Some friends have asked whether I am truly sad to be stepping aside, but I can honestly say that since the announcement I have felt nothing but joy. This is not because I am tired, fed up, unhappy or disgruntled with my job - quite the reverse - but because I am handing on before I get to that point. I am thrilled to hand on to someone who will do a brilliant job and I know the work will be safe in his hands. I have been gifted to build the foundations of the house but Paul is gifted to build the walls. I believe he will do a better job of taking the work forward than I could have done. So it will not crumble away once I am gone but go from strength to strength. Also I feel that the Holy Spirit has begun to prepare me for a new adventure which will be revealed to me in due course. It is actually a great privilege to be able to raise up a Timothy in the House and then hand on to him at the right moment.

A few people might be surprised when I say that I believe Paul will do a better job of taking the work forward than I could have done. Some may mistakenly believe we are in competition. We are not at all and I am confident he will excel. I am not in any way threatened by the gifts of others. I rejoice in the abundant wealth of talent that surrounds me. Their riches are mine also.

I have had some fascinating chats with people about this process, such as the person who came to me and said: 'Don't you think Paul is ever so young for senior leadership?' I replied: 'How old were you when you became managing director of your firm?' He said: 'About 31, I think.' I said: 'That is about the age Paul will be when he takes over.' As I said this the light of understanding entered my friend's eyes and he laughed: 'Oh yes, of course.' It is good to remind ourselves that Jesus was only in His early thirties when He <u>finished</u> his leadership. It is why St Paul said to Timothy:

> *'Don't let anyone look down on you because you are young.'*
> (Timothy 4:12 NIV)

I think leadership teams can make the mistake of raising the bar to entry to their ranks to the level they have achieved after years of experience. That is far too high, and they can forget that, when they were invited into leadership, the bar was much lower. Leadership is not an exclusive club which becomes ever more difficult to enter. The young and the inexperienced need their chance, and they will shine if they are mentored and supported properly.

Several people have asked what I will do when Paul changes things, or makes a decision I would not have made. My reply is that if Paul does not change things then he is not worth a light. Paul must change things because that is the whole point of appointing him. As a baby boomer my style will become increasingly irrelevant to the generation Y which is rising; not so Paul. The church must press on; it must continue to present the Gospel in ways that people can access. To stand still is to decline.

Paul and the many guys of his generation who surround him are the hope for the continuation of the work. They will do well and the work will prosper in their hands.

So what remains for me and Suzy? She has remained at my side through all these years, battling her disease but a constant source of support and encouragement. She has an indomitable spirit and continues to serve, mainly, these days, through mentoring and advising people (she likes to talk!). Her contribution is outstanding and her example is inspirational. For me it does feel as if a new, blank page is turning in the book of our lives and a fresh adventure is fast approaching. From a personal point of view it has been really important to announce I am stepping aside because I need to let go of the old to make room for the new. As I write these words in the spring of 2011 I sense that the Holy Spirit is awakening a renewed passion in me for evangelism. Maybe as the shackles of responsibility for leading a large church are gradually released I will gain a new freedom to preach the Gospel. It is a future to which we both turn with eager anticipation.

Chapter 25

One at a time

As I have previously intimated, one of the key questions we have to address as we try to make new disciples of Jesus Christ is how to get people over the cultural barrier to a place where they can access the truth about Jesus. In Paul's crucial passage about cultural relevance (1Cor 9:19-27) there is a key verse:

> 'I have become all things to all men so that by all possible means I might save some.' (NIV)

What is the main thrust of Paul's message here?

Although he has free will and authority he has deliberately made himself a slave to the needs of all persons and has accommodated himself to various groups for the sake of winning them into God's Kingdom. He does this in order to win people into the Kingdom one at a time, because each person is precious. We should take note:

- He is prepared to reach all sorts of people without prejudice, whatever their background.
- He is prepared to change his approach to suit others so they might understand the Gospel and be able to relate to it, thus helping them over the cultural barrier.

- He understands the necessity of moving towards people rather than expecting them to move towards him.
- He puts his own needs and preferences to the bottom of the pile, subjugating his own likes and dislikes for the sake of others.

We can learn such a lot from this. When we Christians come to church, sometimes our own personal wants, likes and dislikes can all too readily surface if we allow them to. So we become complainers: 'I didn't like that song'; 'I prefer different music'; 'the message was too intellectual'; 'the message was too short'; 'I like formality'; 'I want informality'…and so on *ad nauseam*. It can become all 'me, me, me…' but Paul was all 'them, them, them…' If we want the Kingdom to grow and prosper in this land, we must forget about ourselves and concentrate on the mission of saving some by any possible means.

We can also be reminded that you can have good motives, but bad strategy, and so fail. Our motive can be like Paul's (verse 19) to win as many as possible, but lose out because our message is not dressed in the right clothes so people do not understand us.

I believe we should also remind ourselves why we are working so hard to share the Gospel and run churches. It is for love, because He first loved us.

'For God so loved the world…' (John 3:16 NIV)

Our friends, family, colleagues, neighbours and fellow citizens are truly lost without Jesus, and I believe all Christians should be intentional about doing whatever it takes to try to win them into the Kingdom.

I love the 'Message' Bible version of these verses from 1 Corinthians 9:

'Even though I am free of the demands and expectations of everyone, I have voluntarily become a servant to any and all in order to reach a wide range of people: religious, nonreligious, meticulous moralists, loose-living immoralists, the defeated, the demoralized—whoever. I didn't take on their way of life. I kept my bearings in Christ—but I entered their world and tried to experience things from their point of view. I've become just about every sort of servant there is in my attempts to lead those I meet into a God-saved life. I did all this because of the message. I didn't just want to talk about it; I wanted to be in on it!
You've all been to the stadium and seen the athletes race. Everyone runs; one wins. Run to win. All good athletes train hard. They do it for a gold medal that tarnishes and fades. You're after one that's gold eternally.
I don't know about you, but I'm running hard for the finish line. I'm giving it everything I've got. I'm not going to get caught napping, telling everyone else all about it and then missing out myself.'

I particularly love the phrase: *'I entered their world.'* It gives us the key guidance to what our personal strategy should be, because Jesus entered our world. He humbled Himself, became a slave and was obedient to death on the cross to win our salvation. (Philippians 2) What greater love is there than this?

I want to advocate a strategy for soul winning which I believe will be successful in the 21st Century and which I hope has come loud and clear through the pages of this book. I couch it in terms of a series of searching questions we Christians should ask ourselves:

Finding common ground

Am I surrendering my personal preferences for the sake of winning someone?

Am I entering other people's worlds for the sake of the Gospel?

Am I prepared to make a personal sacrifice for the sake of others?

Am I prepared to be all things to all men in order to win someone, but without compromise on moral issues?

Am I willing to refuse to major on minor issues to help keep the church focussed on what really matters?

Humility

Will I avoid a 'know it all' attitude, calmly listening to people as they tell their story so that here will be no Bible bashing in my personal witness?

Will I be prepared to engage in thoughtful, calm debate, even if sometimes others are aggressive?

Will I help people to know they are loved and accepted?

Am I prepared to form genuine friendships with people who are outside my church friendship group?

Relevance.

Will I avoid street preaching and door knocking, which most people find intrusive due to the incessant bombardment of us all by advertising and cold calling?

Do I realise people really dislike the confrontational approach?

Will I make it my business to find out what cultural language people find difficulty in accessing and be determined not to use it?

Will I become passionate about sharing the Good News relevantly?

Seizing opportunities.

Will I choose not to be silent when the moment arrives and the Holy Spirit prompts me to speak out?

Will I reach out both with kind deeds and bold words to confirm my faith in Jesus?

Do I know that random acts of kindness and words of witness are both weapons in my armoury?

Am I aware that God has the key to someone's heart and I can pray and ask Him to reveal it to me?

Sharing your story

Do I have my personal testimony ready to share, because this is the most powerful way to reach a person's heart?

Can I tell someone not only how I became a Christian, but how He is real in my life at the moment because I have a living faith which is evident to all?

Some readers may say: 'I have heard all this before.' That is good, but are you a doer of the word and not just a hearer? Where is the fruit in your own life? Who has come to faith in Jesus because of your witness? If there is none, then maybe we need to keep on hearing this message again and again until the penny drops, because no strategy is any good unless we put it in to practice. Did you once have a passion to share the Good news, perhaps in your youth, but you have lost it somewhere on the journey? It can be regained by a deliberate act of will, choosing like Paul, to become all things to all men in order to win some.

Here is a wonderful story of someone whose life has been transformed by her encounter with Jesus. It illustrates the point perfectly.

Joanna Day's personal testimony.

What does the Potters House mean to me? Lots! Let me explain. My marriage of 20 years had finally come to an end after years of not working. I was working under intense pressure as the school I work in was in special measures. I had had periods in my life when things looked bleak but never as bleak as this. No happy retirement with a loving partner, simply a life that screamed 'alone.' I was beginning to ask myself: 'Is that it then?' – The end of my life. The end of anything to look forward to – would I simply shrivel and die? I had just made one last rapprochement to my husband to work things out (this was one of many over the years; it usually ended up in a screaming match). I had reached rock bottom.

It was while I was driving along Birches Head Road that I saw a banner on the Bridge Centre. 'Is this all there is to life? Alpha Course. September 29th 2010.' It seemed to hold some of the questions that were going around my head. I was unsure who to contact but I knew my neighbours Stan and Becky. There had been a number of incidents that had meant we came into lots of contact and as I grew to know them better we began to become friends. I knew they attended the Potters House, I had always marvelled and admired how happy they were, how content and always so beautifully human. I asked Becky about the course and she actually apologised for not being able to attend with me every week! Before the course began Becky invited me to the services at the Potters House.

I was brought up as a Roman Catholic and attended a Roman Catholic Grammar School. Both my daughters attended Roman Catholic schools. I have a degree in theology and I have always had an intellectual belief in God and tried to run my life according to Christ's principles and conduct myself with integrity. My first experience of a service at the Potters House was like nothing I had ever experienced in my life! I felt wrapped by a cocoon of love and compassion. The Alpha Course was an incredible experience – I met many people who I now consider friends as well as beginning to understand from the heart the Christian message; all my favourite theologians were mentioned and as I listened it was if I was hearing and seeing the words I knew from a totally different perspective.

The Alpha away day was a turning point. The speaker explained that to truly know Christ you had to forgive. It was like a thunderbolt! One of my very big faults is that I bear grudges. It takes a lot to enrage me but once enraged; I stay enraged! I never forget – or forgive. I knew I needed to forgive and acknowledge my part in the collapse of my marriage. As the old Spanish proverb says "There are three sides to every argument. Yours. Theirs. Somewhere in between there is the truth." It was as if a great burden was rolling off me and when I got home I felt lighter.

I continued to attend the services after Alpha, I also began to be involved on a duty rota but sadly this was sporadic due to the pressures of work. I was also enthusiastically invited to attend a Life Group. What a life affirming experience! I am very lucky to know such brave and wonderful people all of whom have their own stories to tell. The support and camaraderie is such an amazing feeling; I was beginning to understand what it meant to be a Christian in The Potters House. No hypocrisy. No judgement. No ritual. Simply love, compassion, reaching out to the broken and leading by example.

Becky and Stan have been with me constantly, words of encouragement, genuine friendship and genuine understanding, popping through my letterbox little cards reminding me of God's love and, for me, a great gift; Joyce Meyer's The Secret Gift. It is now my armoury at the start and end of a day!

I could go on – and will! The pastoral care team who took me under their wing (possibly one day I could learn to do for someone what was done for me). Finally the New Christian Group that was now being run, not to hit targets or to make a profit, but for me! How incredible is that? When I truly learned from this group the real meaning of Christ's sacrifice these words from Garcia's poem (and immortalised by the singer Leonard Cohen) came to mind:

'And I'll bury my soul in a scrap book, the photographs there and the moss.' I had buried my soul in the struggle to almost single handedly run a home, being the principle wage earner, bring up children, teach and survive. I had walked in the shadows long enough and at that point I gave my life to Jesus freely and gladly. How could I not?

Doors had been clanged shut seemingly leaving me with nothing. As I write this today I feel that I am blessed. This morning Lila (my beautiful large British blue cat) presented me with a battered, torn butterfly. I put the poor injured creature on a peony bud unsure if it was dead or not. It had closed black wings and was crumpled and torn. A few hours later I went out to see the butterfly on the bud with its crumpled wings outstretched. It was noble and beautiful and ready to fly...............

Thank you Becky and Stan. Thank you Potters House. My life is not over. It is a new beginning; I stand here battered and torn but ready to fly. It is a new beginning. To go back to the original question: 'Is this all there is to life?' Absolutely not!

Chapter 26

Fishers of men

In January 2010 I shared my customary New Year message which contained a motto. I have been dreaming up a rhyming motto for a number of years as part of my vision casting strategy and some people have even started taking bets on what it would be (joke!). This particular year it was: 'Born again in twenty ten'. It was a simple reminder to refocus the church on the main purpose of our existence which is to make new disciples of Jesus.

Karl's story

I was 10 years old when I smoked my first cigarette. A friend used to steal them from his Mum's purse and we'd run off into a nearby alley way to smoke them. If we couldn't find any cigarettes, we'd take whisky from the drinks cabinet and mix it with Coca-Cola. Within 12 months, I was smoking regularly and began experimenting with cannabis. Throughout high school, I hung around with older people, who encouraged me to drink and smoke more heavily. We had a love for alcohol and a love for football. I quickly developed a new way of life that was centred on going to football matches, getting drunk and looking for trouble. Not many of us had both parents around when we were growing up and so we looked out for one another. This was where we found acceptance and security.

Somehow, I managed to pass some of my exams and, at 16, went on to college. I lasted six weeks. Most days I would walk into classes drunk or at least hung-over. Despite this, I passed my driving test, found work with a local floor laying company and started a relationship. I'd been friends with her during high school and had always fancied her. I managed to build up the courage to ask her out and was pretty surprised when she said yes! She kept asking me to go with her to a youth group every Friday evening but I always said no. Friday nights were for drinking and preparing myself for 'football.' But she was persistent. One week, most of my friends were tied up with other things and so, just to keep her quiet, I agreed to go.

I'll never forget the first time I went. One of the male leaders came up to me within minutes of me arriving and introduced himself. He was polite and friendly. I didn't understand why and was immediately suspicious of him. But as the conversation went on, I realised he was just a nice lad. I didn't expect to meet people like that and so I struck a deal with my girlfriend: I would go with her to youth group as long as I could go to the pub afterwards. Week by week, I got to know a few of the lads at the youth group. I was shocked to discover that they weren't weird, Bible-bashing freaks. They were like me. They talked about football and cars and other things that I liked talking about.

On one Friday evening, there was a special guest speaker. His name was Craig Marsh and he had an amazing story about how God had changed his life. He talked about his time in the army – how he used to drink, smoke and swear. I really related to what he was saying because I'd been part of the Cadets and had always fancied joining the army myself. The more he talked, the more interested I was. I tried to tell myself that this sort of thing couldn't happen to someone like me but I had strange feeling in my stomach. My hands were sweaty and my heart was beating really fast. At the end of his talk, he asked if anyone would like to find out more about God for themselves. I didn't want to respond. I wanted to leave. Craig began describing how the Holy Spirit can move in your heart and then he started to pray. As he prayed, I felt something that I had never experienced ever before. I felt peace, like I was floating, and as my eyes were closed, I kept seeing really bright colours. It was better than any drug I'd ever taken and so I raised my hand. Afterwards I sat with the youth leader and prayed a prayer to accept Jesus as my Lord and Saviour.

When I left that night, I went to meet my friends in the pub. I couldn't stop thinking about what had happened and what I had experienced. To my amazement, I felt sick when I held a cigarette and I couldn't finish a single pint! I didn't understand what was going on but knew that it had something to do with what I had experienced at the youth group. Ever since that first night, everyone I know has seen a change in me, especially my family. I started going to church and really enjoyed it. The music was good, the speaker was funny and interesting, and all the lads from the youth group were there. I've developed a passion for working with young people and love sharing my story with them. I quit smoking and heavy drinking but best of all, I got a job at the football stadium as a senior steward! My life couldn't have changed any more than it has done. It's amazing and I love it.

In Luke 5:1-11 there is a very vivid story of Jesus and the disciples making a marvellous catch of fish. It is worthy of close analysis because it helps us to understand the urgency of disciple making.

The nets

*'...left there by the fishermen, who were **washing their nets**.'*

The nets had to be kept in good condition, washed to remove weeds and mended. It was their livelihood; if they didn't look after their kit, they couldn't fish, then they would starve. This reminds me that if we don't fish for souls the church will starve spiritually. There is no spiritual social security. Fishing is the lifeblood of the church. The nets were bell shaped, with weights attached, and they were thrown flat onto the water over a shoal, then hauled in to capture the fish. This suggests to me that the net does **not discriminate**, that all are welcome. In other words, the love of God extends to all people regardless of their social or racial background.

Fish move in shoals

*'**Put out** into deep water, and let down the nets for a catch.'*

Jesus is effectively saying: 'over there, that's where the fish are!' It reminds me that people are generally gregarious; we like to be together in groups. Worship, preaching and physical environment are crucial factors and form a framework for successful Kingdom work, but I think the biggest single factor in whether or not a person comes or stays in church is **friendship.** I think many people are just waiting to be asked to come to church and they are looking for a friend to bring them. It is a very successful strategy to try to bring a friend to an Alpha course or similar event. Where we put on bridging type events like concerts and parties and encourage Christians to bring their friends, I think we will find many fish willing to jump into the net. This has to be accompanied by an intentional strategy of offering a warm welcome to new friends and creating friendship groups which are open. Church needs to have the feel of a place that welcomes strangers rather than a private club which is difficult to access.

Look out not in

*'Simon answered, "Master, we've worked hard **all night...**"'*

My thought here is that Simon had fished in darkness, which perhaps could be an illustration of being absorbed with self. **Looking inward** is not the way of the Christian. It is all too easy to lose focus and become self absorbed. It is helpful to do a reality check from time to time and make sure we are looking to the needs of others first. Jesus brought light and revelation. He snapped them out of it.

Beware the prideful response

> *"'...and haven't caught anything...'"*

I think Peter is saying: 'who are you to tell us what to do? What do you know about fishing?'

We need to be careful of making such a response to God. **He always knows what is best**. He sees the secret place in a person's heart, he knows if they are ready to hear the Gospel.

Follow His instructions

> *"'...But because you say so, I will let down the nets." When they had done so, they caught such a large number of fish that their nets began to break.'*

At the Potter's House we have encouraged the congregation to employ the following evangelism strategy:

- Be intentional about cultivating some friendships with people who are unchurched. Offer genuine friendship which continues whether or not the person shows any interest in church.
- Pray for them privately.
- Offer to pray for and with them when they are facing a difficult situation.
- Be nice to them and enjoy social or sporting activities with them.
- Talk about Jesus naturally.
- Invite and bring to a church event when it seems the right moment.

- Above all follow the guidance of the Holy Spirit.
- And absolutely no Bible bashing.

The net that the disciples cast did not catch all the fish that were living in the Sea of Galilee.

This might seem an obvious point but it is an illustration of the fact that each person has free will…each person must choose whether or not to respond to the Gospel. **All we believers are asked to do is to fish**, and leave the rest to them and to Him.

When we work together

> 'So **they signalled their partners** in the other boat to come and help them, and they came and filled both boats so full that they began to sink.'

Where there is unity and cooperation I believe we create the right conditions for the Kingdom to grow. It must always be **a partnership**. The church provides the environment, the people do the fishing. So the church puts on an Alpha course and we all try to bring someone.

There will be surprises

> 'For he and all his companions were **astonished** at the catch of fish they had taken…'

Sometimes the person we think is least ready is the one who makes the positive response.

For example: in casual conversation you drop that you go to church. Your friend says:' I'd like to go to church, can I come with you?' You bring them; after only a few short weeks they make their decision to follow Jesus. You are astonished and delighted.

Why does the unexpected happen? It's because there are seasons in our lives and sometimes people are just ready to respond to Jesus. They are like **a ripe fruit waiting** to be plucked from the vine.

If we are not in the habit of gently fishing we can miss opportunities like these.

We are all fishers of men

> *'Then Jesus said to Simon, "Don't be afraid; from now on you will **catch men.**"'*

It is so important to grasp this point because **evangelism cannot be left to the evangelist**, whose job it is merely to harvest the seeds which have already been sown by others. I am an evangelist and I can preach the Gospel, but there is no point to doing so if there is no audience of unchurched people who want to listen to me. I will not be friends with, or meet these people on a day to day basis and it is solely the responsibility of each individual Christian to do this introductory work with their friends.

I think on average Christians may have at least 10 people they know reasonably well who don't come to church, such as colleagues, family, neighbours and friends. So that is ten times the number of people who come to a church. We have a much bigger shoal than we imagine.

It's time to fish

> *'So they pulled their boats up on shore, left everything **and followed him.**'*

I guess we all know of someone who always has a project on the go and in the shed is a partly sanded old chair they are doing up, or in the garage a half finished kit car. I know people are more precious than mere projects, but I think **we should all have a person** we are praying for and working on; a project on the go.

Have we?

It's time to be about the Lord's business. God is passionate about His fish, His people. The mission is urgent, the opportunity is all around us. Fish undergo a transformation during the fishing process. They die after they are caught; then they are born again into a delicious meal for the master's banquet. It is a parable about how all Christians could and should be involved in the miraculous work of salvation.

Where the Gospel is preached and people are encouraged to make a personal commitment to Jesus and His Way…
Where the Gospel is preached relevantly so that people in the 21st Century can understand and connect with it…
Where hurts are healed…
Where there is clear vision…
Where there is strong leadership…

Where there is teamwork and people are empowered, trained, mentored and released…

Where there is prevailing prayer…

Where the Holy Spirit is allowed to move freely…

Where ordinary Christians take hold of their responsibility to witness…

…the Kingdom will grow and the church will prosper.

The priority must be to make new disciples of Jesus Christ. Numbers matter, they really do. The call to be fishers of men has never been as urgent as now and I believe that all Christians should heed the call.

We are all fishers of men.*

---

*Although in Luke 5:10 Jesus specifically refers to catching 'men', I prefer to think of the word in its generic sense, that is, humankind; people, men and women.

Acknowledgements

Sincere thanks to:

    Ron Willoughby for giving me much encouragement to write this story

    Brian Barber and Emma Jenkinson for their hard work in editing the original text

    Paul Nixon and Rob Phillips for reading the script and giving helpful comments

    Sam Taylor for designing the cover

    The army of volunteers who have given so much to the cause of advancing God's Kingdom

The cover illustration is an original picture by Rik Berry and is reproduced with kind permission. You can find more of Rik's beautiful pictures at Brush of the Wind Gallery, http://valleygate.getmyip.com/rikberry/ or via email at rik@rikberry.com

Pastor Phil Barber may be contacted at:
phil.barber@thebridgecentre.org.uk

The Potter's House:
The Bridge Centre
Birches Head Road
Stoke-on-Trent
ST2 8DD
United Kingdom

Tel: +44 (0) 1782 683781

www.thepottershouse.eu